ROUGH GUIDES

T0019847

POCKET **ROUGH GUIDE**
ISTANBUL

written and researched by
TERRY RICHARDSON

CONTENTS

ISTANBUL

Few of the world's cities capture the imagination quite like Istanbul, superbly situated at the confluence of predominantly Christian Europe and the largely Muslim Middle East. It is a booming megalopolis of more than fifteen million people, standing astride both the Asian and European sides of the Bosphorus strait, the vibrant cultural and economic powerhouse of a resurgent Turkish Republic. Of course, Istanbul has been a major city for over two thousand years, and it is the incredible legacy of the two great empires which made it their capital, the Christian Byzantines and Muslim Ottoman Turks, that make it so appealing today.

Rüstem Paşa Camii

The makings of a perfect kebab

For most visitors, Istanbul is a city of two, albeit rather uneven, halves. The first is the old city, strategically located on a peninsula pointing east across the Bosphorus towards Asia, and cut-off from the European mainland to the west by the substantial remains of the monumental Byzantine-era land walls. The peninsula is bound to the south by the glimmering waters of the Sea of Marmara, to the north by the curving inlet of one of the world's finest natural harbours, the Golden Horn. Like ancient Rome, which Constantinople superseded as the Roman Empire's major city, it was built on seven hills. There is so much to see and do in the old city that you could spend weeks exploring its many sights, but even with just a few days at your disposal it's possible to get a real flavour of this great metropolis.

Best places for a perfect kebab

Forget that soggy late-night kebab at your local takeaway. Real kebabs come in many forms in the land of their birth and eating them is a seriously enjoyable business. Try a metre-long special at *Akdeniz Hatay Sofrası* (see page 70), a lunchtime stand-up treat at *Dönerci Şahin Üsta* (see page 68), a southeast Turkish delight at *Develi* (see page 83) or a *rakı*-enhanced kebab feast at *Kenan Üsta Ocakbaşı* (see page 106).

The second half of the city is the European quarter of Beyoğlu and Galata, north across the Golden Horn from the old city and easily reached by tram or metro. As well as being home to the famous Galata Tower and a host of wonderful, mainly nineteenth-century buildings, it is Istanbul's entertainment hub. Even if you've no interest in the hedonistic delights of cinema-going, gallery-gazing, shopping, bar-hopping, puffing on a water pipe or clubbing, you should come here to challenge your preconceptions of what a predominantly Muslim city is like, dine at one of the myriad (usually excellent) restaurants or simply join the Friday or Saturday crush of people surging down İstiklal Caddesi. Then, if there's time, a bargain ferry ride to Asia awaits.

Drinking and dining in Beyoğlu

Fortunately, the majority of the major sights, such as the Haghia Sophia (Aya Sofya), Topkapı Palace and Blue Mosque, are located within a short distance of each other in compact Sultanahmet. By far the best way to explore is on foot, especially as there are so many smaller, easily missed sights tucked-in between the major ones, from Byzantine cisterns to historic Turkish baths. The buzzing waterfront around the Golden Horn-spanning Galata Bridge is unmissable, and offers superb views up to the old city's exotic skyline of domes and slender minarets. Try, too, to get a taste of the conservative parts of the old city by walking a section of the land walls or exploring the backstreets of the northwest quarter. Although the language barrier may be formidable and street signage less than perfect, don't be afraid to wander off the beaten path and temporarily mislay yourself. After all, with water on three sides and the towering land walls on the fourth you'll eventually reach an unmissable landmark.

When to visit

Hot, humid summers and cold, damp winters mean spring and autumn are the best times to visit, with May–June and September–October offering the (usually) dry, warm weather ideal for exploring on foot. Needless to say, this is also the most expensive time for accommodation. Midsummer is more than bearable, however, with maximum temperatures rarely exceeding 28 degrees – avoid long tramps during the hottest part of the day and enjoy the benefits of warm evenings in a rooftop bar or restaurant. One downside of midsummer visits is that many Istanbulites decamp to Aegean resorts and some clubs close for the duration. Winters can be snowy, most likely in January or February, or more usually simply cold, wet and windy (the downside of the city's proximity to so much water means it has a maritime climate). Fog can also be a problem in winter, sometimes closing the Bosphorus to shipping. On the plus side, hotel rates are cheaper and the arts and cultural scene vibrant.

Where to...

Shop

With some four thousand shops in a mall over five hundred years old, the **Grand Bazaar** should not be missed. There's everything from fake designer jeans to centuries-old Turkish rugs and plenty of cafés to take the weight off your feet. The **Spice Bazaar** in Eminönü is more manageable and equally historic, while the streets around it are wonderful for foodstuffs. The **Arasta Bazaar** near the Blue Mosque is good for quality souvenirs; for more food shopping, head to **Kadıköy** in Asia or into conservative Fatih for the Çarşamba Pazarı (Wednesday Bazaar). For fashion, go to **İstiklal Caddesi**.
OUR FAVOURITES: Istanbul Handicrafts Centre see page 55, Tatlıcı Safa see page 55, Historia Mall see page 68

Drink

Turkey may be predominantly Muslim, but there are plenty of places to enjoy a drink in Istanbul. The most lively area by far is buzzing **Galata/Beyoğlu**, where student bars rub shoulders with hip licensed cafés and the well-heeled sip cocktails at expensive rooftop establishments. **Nevizade Sokak** in Beyoğlu is particularly noted for its raucous drinking (and eating) scene, particularly madcap on a Friday and Saturday night. The old city is much quieter, though there are plenty of places on Divan Yolu and Akbıyık Caddesi for a beer, glass of wine or the national drink, *rakı*, an aniseed spirit.
OUR FAVOURITES: Balkon see page 108, Fes Cafe see page 69, Mila see page 125

Eat

Istanbulites are fussy and demanding when it comes to food. Whether choosing a humble *simit* (sesame-coated bread ring) from a street barrow or a freshly caught fish in a stylish Bosphorus-front restaurant, they'll only accept the best. Fish is highly prized, but you'll also find all kinds of *sulu yemek* (stews), Turkish "pizzas" *pide* and *lahmacun*, savoury pies and breads, soups and, of course, kebabs – either grilled over charcoal at an *ocakbaşı* or sliced off a rotating spit at a *dönerci*. However tempting, avoid dining in tourist-dominated Sultanahmet and instead head to **Galata/Beyoğlu** or across to **Asia**.
OUR FAVOURITES: Hatay Sofrası see page 70, Karaköy Lokantası see page 92, Mikla see page 107

Go Out

The old city has very little in the way of nightlife. The real action is across the Golden Horn, primarily in and around İstiklal Caddesi in Beyoğlu, where there are clubs catering to every taste, from hard rock to dance and jazz to blues. **Galata** has a few small bohemian venues, as does Kadıköy in **Asia**. For pop glitz, head down to the Bosphorus-front in **Ortaköy/Kuruçeşme**. For something more Turkish, try a *meyhane*, a kind of tavern where the food (usually fish) takes second place to drink and the locals sing and dance to traditional music.
OUR FAVOURITES: Nardis Jazz Club see page 93, Fosil see page 93, Limoncello see page 117

Istanbul at a glance

Galata and the waterfront districts p.84.
Vibrant bohemian quarter famed for its landmark tower and fabulous views to the old city.

HASKÖY

KASİMPAŞA

GALATASA

GALATA

BEYO

KARAK

GOLDEN HORN

Northwest quarter and the land walls p.72.
Wander the atmospheric backstreets of the city's most conservative quarter, or along the six kilometres of the most successful fortification ever built.

FATIH

ZEYREK

SÜLEYMANIYE

AKSARAY

KUMKAPI

Grand Bazaar District p.58.
A fascinating quarter centred on a sprawling fifteenth-century shopping mall and sublime hilltop mosque.

| 0 | metres | 500 |
| 0 | yards | 500 |

Sultanahmet p.24.
The heart of the historic old city, ideal for exploring on foot.

HARBIYE

MAÇKA

BEŞİKTAŞ

TAKSİM

DOLMABAHÇE

ÇİHANGİR

KABATAŞ

ÇUKURCUMA

TOPHANE

Beşiktaş and Ortaköy p.112.
A swanky Bosphorus-front district,
home to historic palaces and glitzy clubs.

Beyoğlu and Taksim p.94.
The metropolis's entertainment hub, this is
the place to wine, dine, club, shop and take in
a gallery or two.

BOSPHORUS

ÜSKÜDAR

İNÖNÜ

Topkapı Palace to the Golden Horn p.42.
Encompasses a walled palace complex,
great museum, period railway station
and bustling waterfront.

HAREM

CANKURTARAN

Asian Istanbul p.118.
Shuttle across the Bosphorus on a
commuter ferry to mosque-studded
Üsküdar or bustling Kadıköy.

**SEA OF
MARMARA**

▽ **The Bosphorus & Princes' Islands** p.126.
A boat ride up the Bosphorus, or out to the
pine-scented Princes' Islands, makes for an
ideal getaway from Istanbul's hustle and bustle.

15

Things not to miss

It's not really possible to see everything that Istanbul has to offer in one trip – and we don't suggest you try. What follows is a selective taste of their highlights – from fantastic architecture to charming markets.

< **Mosaic Museum Büyük**
See page 31
Charming collection of mosaics from the long-gone Byzantine Great Palace.

∨ **Church of the Pammakaristos**
See page 75
A typical late-Byzantine church-turned-mosque adorned with stunning mosaics.

< **Haghia Sophia**
See page 25
The most important church of the Byzantine world was converted into a mosque in 1453 and to a museum in 1934.

∨ **Istanbul Modern**
See page 87
The name says it all, a real contrast to the sights of the old city.

∧ Grand Bazaar
See page 59
This fifteenth-century covered market boasts 66 streets and over 4000 shops – the ultimate mall.

< Ayasofya Hürrem
See page 30
Ottoman hamams were temples to hygiene, godliness and gossip.

∧ **Galata Tower**
See page 84
Gaze across the busy waters of the Golden Horn to the exotic skyline of the old city.

∨ **360 bar-restaurant**
See page 107
This swanky rooftop establishment delivers what its name promises – at a price.

∧ Street cart snacks
See page 24
Sesame-coated bagels, roast chestnuts and sweetcorn are among the goodies pushed around Sultanahmet's streets.

< Spice Bazaar
See page 52
A centuries-old waterfront bazaar packed with spices, herbs and Turkish delight.

< **İstiklal Caddesi**
See page 94
High-street shops, historic
arcades, a mall and much more.

∨ **Bosphorus cruise**
See page 126
A bargain ferry ride up the
continent-dividing Bosphorus
strait is a great day out.

Day One in Istanbul

Haghia Sophia. See page 25. The mosaic-clad interior of the domed Haghia Sophia (Aya Sofya), for a thousand years the largest enclosed space in the world, still impresses today.

Basilica Cistern. See page 24. Beautifully lit and atmospheric underground Byzantine cistern, famed for its Medusa-head carvings and lazy carp.

Lunch. See page 38. Grilled meatballs are a Turkish favourite, and *Tarihi Sultanahmet Köftecisi*, overlooking the heart of the old city, does them to perfection.

Haghia Sophia

Blue Mosque. See page 34. With its cascade of domes and plethora of gorgeous blue tiles from which its name derives, the Blue Mosque is unmissable.

Hippodrome. See page 33. A relatively tranquil square, this was in Roman and Byzantine times a chariot-racing circuit, dominated by the splendid Egyptian Obelisk.

Sokollu Mehmet Paşa Camii. See page 32. A beautiful Ottoman mosque tucked away in the backstreets near the Hippodrome.

Church of St Sergius and Bacchus. See page 31. Below the Hippodrome, this former early-Byzantine church is today the Little Haghia Sophia (Küçük Aya Sofya Camii), a working mosque.

Basilica Cistern

Dinner. See page 40. Sample a multitude of delicious cold and hot *meze* morsels (starters) at *Giritli* before a fish main, washed down, if you go for the fixed-meal deal, with an unlimited amount of wine, *rakı* or beer.

Giritli

Day Two in Istanbul

Topkapı Palace. See page 43.
Make an early start to explore
this fascinating palace complex,
ranged around a series of attractive
courtyard gardens.

Archeology Museum. See page
42. Receiving far less attention
than it deserves, this fine museum
exhibits a wealth of artefacts from
the former Ottoman domains.

Lunch. See page 56. Grab
a fish sandwich from *Tarihi
Eminönü Balık Ekmek* and enjoy
the vibrant chaos of Eminönü
waterfront.

Topkapı Palace

Spice Bazaar. See page 52.
Admire the beautifully arranged
spices for sale in this covered
Ottoman market – but make
your purchases in the streets
round about.

Rüstem Paşa Camii. See page
54. A gem of a mosque in
the bustling bazaar quarter of
Eminönü, noted for its gorgeous
İznik tiles.

Coffee. See page 68. After
toiling up the third hill, stop
in the "hidden" *Ağa Kapısı* café for
incomparable views down to the
Galata Bridge and Bosphorus.

Archeology Museum

Süleymaniye Külliyesi. See page
58. This mosque complex is
the masterwork of the Ottomans'
greatest architect – unmissable.

Süleymaniye Hamamı. See page
59. Part of the mosque complex;
unwind after your heavy day in this
steamy and attractive hamam.

Dinner. See page 40. For
kebabs made with various
meats, *Şirvan Sofrası*, a popular
place in the Sultanahmet district,
is perfect.

Spice Bazaar

Backstreet Istanbul

The biggest and best concentration of traditional backstreets is in the conservative northwest quarter. Winding their way along the old city's fourth, fifth and sixth hills, they are home to many seldom-visited sights and afford great views.

Aqueduct of Valens. See page 66. You can't miss the two-tiered arches of this Byzantine engineering marvel spanning traffic-clogged Atatürk Bulvarı.

Yavuz Selim Camii. See page 75. Beautifully austere imperial mosque atop the old city's fifth hill, offering grand views over the Golden Horn.

Church of the Pammakaristos. See page 75. The funerary chapel of this little-visited Byzantine jewel is today a museum with some fine mosaics.

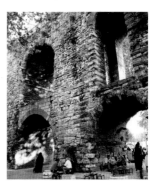
Aqueduct of Valens

Lunch. See page 83. Noted for updated versions of traditional Ottoman dishes, *Asitane* is right next to the Kariye Museum.

The Kariye Museum. See page 72. Every picture tells a story at the former Church of St Saviour in Chora, this mosque houses one of the best collections of Byzantine mosaics anywhere.

The land walls. See page 79. Follow the mighty land walls down to the Golden Horn, past the once-grand Palace of the Porphyrogenitus.

Ferry to Asia. See page 147. A ferry from the jetty at Ayvansaray runs down the Horn and across the Bosphorus to Üsküdar.

Dinner. See page 125. Eat at *Kanaat Lokantası*, a very traditional (and dry) restaurant in conservative Üsküdar.

Asitane

The Kariye Museum

The European quarter

The old city may have all the major historic sights, but for a hint of fin-de-siècle decadence, a generous slice of the contemporary arts, and a no-holds-barred night on the town, try the European quarter.

Istanbul Modern. See page 87. Great introduction to modern Turkish art and plenty of temporary exhibitions at this Bosphorus-front retort to London's Tate Modern.

Galata Tower. See page 84. Ascend to the balcony of this landmark Genoese tower for superb vistas.

🍽 **Lunch**. See page 91. The views from the popular rooftop *Galata Konak* café-cum-patisserie are just wonderful.

Galata Mevlevi Lodge. See page 84. See the hall where the dervishes whirled in this fascinating little museum.

İstiklal Caddesi. See page 94. Formerly the Grand Rue de Pera and lined with fine nineteenth-century buildings, this is the city's premier shopping and entertainment street.

☕ **Tea**. See page 98. The tearooms of the grand *Pera Palace Hotel* are a period delight.

Pera Museum. See page 98. Fine gallery-cum-museum housed in a beautifully restored nineteenth-century building.

🍽 **Dinner**. See page 106. A lively Istanbul-Greek *meyhane* (taverna), *İmroz* is great for a raucous meal out.

Venue. See page 93. *Nardis Jazz Club*, a short hop from the Galata Tower, is a cool and sophisticated venue.

View of the Golden Horn from Galata Tower

İstiklal Caddesi

Tea at the Kubbeli Saloon Lounge, Pera Palace Hotel

PLACES

Tram on İstiklal Caddesi

Sultanahmet

Once the fulcrum of both the Christian Byzantine and Muslim Ottoman empires, Sultanahmet is the heart of old Istanbul. The essence of its grand, imperial past is distilled in two truly great, domed buildings facing each other imperiously over an attractive park – the monumental sixth-century church of Haghia Sophia, today the Aya Sofya, and the equally impressive Blue Mosque, built a thousand years later. There are plenty more notable, historic buildings scattered across the crown of the peninsula and in the old alleys running down to the shipping-filled blue waters of the Sea of Marmara, and you could easily spend two or three days sightseeing in Sultanahmet alone. Inevitably, tourism is Sultanahmet's raison d'être today, and there are legions of hotels, cafés and restaurants catering to visitors' needs.

Milion

MAP P.26, POCKET MAP H11
Divan Yolu ❶ 1 Sultanahmet

Unfortunately, in their rush to get to the nearby Haghia Sophia, most visitors walk by the remains of the Milion without noticing it – hardly surprising, given that it is a mere stump of marble lost in a verge at the eastern end of busy Divan Yolu. This is all that's left of the once-magnificent **triumphal arch** surmounted by a cross, flanked on either side by a statue of the Emperor Constantine and his mother Helena, beneath which was a milestone measuring distances to all corners of the Roman Empire. The crudely built stone tower next to it is actually an Ottoman-era water regulator for the Basilica Cistern (Yerebatan Sarnıcı) below your feet.

Basilica Cistern (Yerebatan Sarnıcı)

MAP P.26, POCKET MAP H11
Yerebatan Cad 1/3 ❶ 1 Sultanahmet
Ⓦ yerebatan.com. Charge, extra for audio guide.

The Yerebatan Sarnıcı or "Sunken Cistern", just downhill from the Milion, is better known to foreigners as the Basilica Cistern. five,,Built originally under Emperor Constantine when he was refounding the city as his new imperial capital, it was much modified in the sixth century. It could hold up to 80,000 cubic metres of water, used to supply the Great Palace of Byzantine-era Constantinople and, in the Ottoman period, the Topkapı Palace. The attractive roof, comprising a series of brick-built domes, is supported by a veritable forest of 336 columns arranged in 12 rows of 28, each topped by a capital, the most attractive of which are of the elaborately carved, acanthus-leaf Corinthian variety. Walkways lead through the columns, allowing visitors to admire the carp swimming in the shallow, clear and subtly illuminated waters, as well as wonder at the massive amount of work its 1987 restoration must have been, when some 50,000 tonnes of mud were dredged out of the 140m long by 70m wide cistern. At the far end of the cistern are two massive capitals, both carved into the form of the snake-haired mythological creature **Medusa** and each supporting a pillar. Almost certainly reused from much earlier structures, one Medusa is upside down, the other laid on its side, possibly because the Medusa was a pagan symbol and the cistern was built in the Christian period. A scene from the 1963 James Bond film *From Russia with Love* was shot here.

Cafer Ağa Theological School (Cafer Ağa Mecresesi)

MAP P.26, POCKET MAP H11
Caferiye Sok ⓣ 1 Sultanahmet ⓣ 0212 513 3601.

In the shadow of the Haghia Sophia, this former Islamic theological school was designed by the prolific Ottoman master architect Sinan in the sixteenth century. The domed rooms ranged around the attractive courtyard, formerly the cells of the theology students, are now home to the studios of craftspeople maintaining traditional Ottoman arts such as *ebru* (marbling), calligraphy and the painting of miniatures. Many of their wares are for sale and the whole enterprise is surprisingly low-key given that it is situated in the most heavily touristed part of the city.

Haghia Sophia (Aya Sofya)

MAP P.26, POCKET MAP H11
Sultanahmet Meydanı 1 ⓣ 1 Sultanahmet ⓦ ayasofyamuzesi.gov.tr. Charge for audio guide.

Representative of the Byzantine Empire at the peak of its power in the sixth century, the Haghia Sophia, or **Church of the Holy Wisdom**, still inspires awe today. Two previous churches of the same name had stood on the site before being razed, the latter in a riot in 532. Justinian, determined to bolster his temporal and spiritual authority, ordered a rebuild on a scale not realized before. The architects, Greek mathematician Anthemius and geometer Isidore, came up with an innovative and much-imitated design – covering a near-square building with a

Basilica Cistern

Sultanahmet

ACCOMMODATION
Agora Guest House & Hostel	16
Alp	10
Cheers	1
Cheers Lighthouse	18
Deniz Houses	17
Empress Zoe	6
Four Seasons Sultanahmet	7
Hanedan	12
Ibrahim Paşa	14
Kybele	4
Nomade	5
Ottoman Hotel Imperial	3
Peninsula	8
Side Hotel & Pension	11
Sultan Hostel	13
Turkoman	15
Uyan	9
White House	2

SHOPS
Chez Galip	4
Cocoon	6
Galeri Kayseri	2
İznik Classics	3
Jennifer's Hamam	5
Yörük Collection	1

CAFÉS
Çiğdem Patisserie	3
Edebiyat Kiraathanesi	5
Tarihi Sultanahmet Köftecisi	6
The Pudding Shop	7

RESTAURANTS
Albura Kathisma	8
Amedros	2
Balıkçı Sabahattin	9
Doy Doy	10
Dubb	4
Giritli	11
Matbah	1
Şirvan Sofrası	12

BARS
Cozy Pub	1
Istanbul Terrace Bar	3
Just Bar	4
Pierre Loti Roof-Bar	2

Haghia Sophia interior

dome of unprecedented height and impressive diameter.

Sunk a few metres below current ground-level at the entrance to Justinian's masterpiece is the stepped base of the second church, along with a series of blocks which once adorned its facade, relief-carved with sheep symbolizing the Twelve Apostles. The so-called "Beautiful Gate", the central door of five, leads to the **inner narthex**, a vaulted vestibule containing the sarcophagus of the Empress Irene. Further doorways lead to the inner narthex, its ceiling glittering with gold mosaics and containing, above the imperial portal leading to the nave, a stunning mosaic panel depicting an all-powerful Christ being beseeched by Emperor Leo IV.

It is the **nave** of the church, however, that is truly inspiring. Here the 32-metre diameter central dome, towering 55 metres above floor level, appears to be suspended in mid-air, its supporting piers cleverly concealed in the twin line of pillars separating the nave from the aisles. Two half-domes join the central dome to the west and east, emphasizing the sense of space,

an effect aided by light filtering in from the forty windows puncturing the dome. Also on the ground floor is the **weeping column**, so-called because it "sweats" water and supposedly cures all ills, and the omphalos, a marble-inlay floor panel where coronations took place.

Following the 1453 Ottoman Turkish conquest of the city, this church became, as the **Aya Sofya Camii**, the city's major mosque. Thus the apse is pierced by a Mecca-facing niche (*mihrab*), flanked to one side by a prayer-platform (*mimber*). There's also the loge, a platform used by the Sultan at Friday prayers, and eight large plaques below the dome adorned with Arabic calligraphy. Outside, the four minarets at each corner of the building were added post-Ottoman conquest. It was turned into the Aya Sofya museum in 1934s.

Reached by a stone ramp from the inner narthex's north end are the **upper galleries**. The south gallery is the most interesting as it contains several beautifully executed and preserved Byzantine mosaic panels, including one depicting John the Baptist and the Virgin Mary beseeching an impassive-looking Christ to save humanity. Scratched into the marble balustrade here is some Viking graffiti, probably scrawled by a member of the Varangian Guard, bodyguards to the Byzantine emperors recruited from Scandinavia. Exiting via the south end of the inner narthex, in the **Vestibule of Warriors**, is the pick of the church's mosaic panels. Executed in the late tenth century, it depicts the Virgin and Child. On her right, Emperor Justinian offers a model of the Haghia Sophia church; to her left, an even more munificent Emperor Constantine presents her with a model of his city, Constantinople.

Soğuk Çeşme Sokağı

MAP P.26, POCKET MAP H11

🚇 1 Sultanahmet.

In Turkish, Soğuk Çeşme Sokağı means "street of the cold fountains", though the cobbled alley is notable today not for its fountains but for the attractively restored nineteenth-century wooden houses lining its cobbled course. It's worth strolling down this pedestrianized lane to see a version of how the old city would have looked before the modern era, when the then-standard wooden houses, subject to frequent fires, were rebuilt in brick and concrete. The houses are attractively painted, with traditional overhanging upper floors.

Fountain of Ahmet III (Ahmet III Çeşmesi)

MAP P.26, POCKET MAP J11

Bab-ı Hümayün Cad 🚇 1 Sultanahmet.

Situated just in front of the Bab-ı Hümayün gateway leading to the outer court of the Topkapı Palace (see page 43), this splendidly ornate, eighteenth-century Turkish Rococo fountain is the most

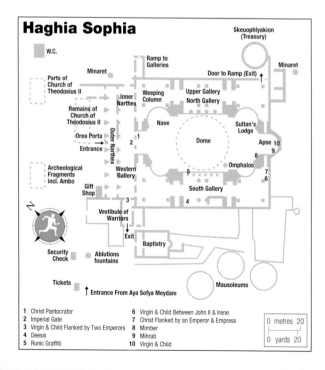

Haghia Sophia

Skeuophlyakion (Treasury)

W.C.

Ramp to Galleries

Minaret

Door to Ramp (Exit)

Minaret

Parts of Church of Theodosius II

Weeping Column

Upper Gallery North Gallery

Inner Narthex

Remains of Church of Theodosius II

Nave

Sultan's Lodge

Orea Porta

Outer Narthex

1

Dome

Apse 10

Entrance

2

8 9

Archeological Fragments incl. Ambo

Western Gallery

5

Omphalos

7

Gift Shop

3

4

South Gallery

6

Vestibule of Warriors

Exit

Baptistry

Security Check

Ablutions fountains

Tickets

↑ Entrance From Aya Sofya Meydanı

Mausoleums

1 Christ Pantocrator	6 Virgin & Child Between John II & Irene
2 Imperial Gate	7 Christ Flanked by an Emperor & Empress
3 Virgin & Child Flanked by Two Emperors	8 Mimber
4 Deesis	9 Mihrab
5 Runic Graffiti	10 Virgin & Child

0 metres 20

0 yards 20

attractive in the city. The building is almost square, with stylized, massively overhanging eaves topped by five small domes. At each corner are counters covered by ornate, curved marble window grilles, from which refreshments such as iced water and sherbets would have been handed to passers-by in the Ottoman period. These water dispensers, known as *sebil* in Turkish, were found throughout the city and often, as here, also had wall-mounted taps (*çeşme*) to provide that most basic of necessities to a local populace whose homes lacked running water.

Carpet Museum (Hali Müzesi)

MAP P.26, POCKET MAP H11
Bab-ı Hümayün Cad ⊕ 1 Sultanahmet
☎ 0212 518 1330. Charge.

Located in the domed soup kitchens attached to the Haghia Sophia (Aya Sofya), the Carpet Museum, opened in 2013, displays a fantastic range of fine carpets and kilims woven between the fourteenth and twentieth centuries. The exhibits, many of them taken from mosques across Anatolian

Turkey, are well labelled, and there is plenty of information both on how the rugs were made and the significance of the patterns with which they are decorated.

Ayasofya Hürrem (Sultan Hamam)

MAP P.26, POCKET MAP H12
Bab-ı Hümayün Cad 1 ⊕ 1 Sultanahmet
Ⓦ ayasofyahamami.com. Charge.

Built by Sinan in 1556 for Sultan Süleyman the Magnificent, appropriately enough on the site of the Roman Baths of Zeuxippus, this beautiful hamam (Turkish baths) was originally intended for the faithful attending the Aya Sofya Camii. It was named after Süleyman's wife, known to Turks as Haseki Hürrem, though better known in the west as Roxelana. In 2011, following many years of restoration, it became a working hamam once again. The building comprises two separate baths, for men and women, with entry from either end into the large, domed *camekan* or reception/changing area. Beyond this lies the main bath chamber, the *hararet*, where bathers sluice themselves down with water

Fountain of Ahmet III

Mosaic in Great Palace Mosaic Museum

from a basin or "steam" on the hot *göbek taşı* ("navel stone").

Mosaic Museum Büyük (Saray Mozaikleri Müzesi)

MAP P.26, POCKET MAP H12
Torun Sok 103 ① 1 Sultanahmet ① 0212 518 1205. Charge.

The mosaics exhibited on the floor in this museum are actually *in situ*, and once formed part of a huge panel adorning the courtyard of one of the royal residences within the Great Palace complex of the Byzantine period, which sprawled all the way down the hill to the Sea of Marmara. Sections have been taken up and wall-mounted to make viewing easier, and some are so finely executed they contain 40,000 *tesserae* (mosaic pieces) per square metre. They depict quite charming scenes from everyday **Byzantine life**. In one, a stubborn goat resists the efforts of a shepherd to drag it along by its tether, in another an equally stubborn donkey turns its head away from a basket of food. Less cute are the hunting dogs bringing down a bloodied hare, leopards feasting on the carcass of an antelope and

a lion tangling messily with an elephant. Although most of the mosaics here probably date from the firmly Christian sixth century, some of the scenes are pagan, Classical-era in nature, including the mythological hero Bellerophon taking on the monstrous fire-breathing Chimera.

Arasta Bazaar

MAP P.26, POCKET MAP H12
Arasta Çarşısı 143 ① 1 Sultanahmet ① 0212 520 4046.

Originally, this long bazaar of small shops was part of the early seventeenth-century Blue Mosque complex and the revenues from it helped pay for upkeep of the mosque. An attractive market area, it's far less hassle to browse here than in the much larger Grand Bazaar. Today, there are 77 shops, selling everything from traditional Turkish carpets and kilims through to İznik tiles and Meerschaum pipes.

Church of St Sergius and Bacchus (Küçük Aya Sofya Camii)

MAP P.26, POCKET MAP G9
Küçük Aya Sofya Cad ① 1 Sultanahmet.

The "small mosque of Aya Sofya", as it is known in Turkish, is presumably so called because of its resemblance, on a miniature scale, to the Aya Sofya itself. It is located down the hill from the Blue Mosque and Arasta Bazaar, close to the Sea of Marmara, and was originally the church for the nearby **Palace of Hormisdas**, a part of the Great Palace complex. Commissioned by Justinian and his consort Theodora, the church slightly predated that of Haghia Sophia, having been begun in 527 and completed in 536. The ground plan of the church is an irregular octagon, with beautiful marble columns supporting an encircling gallery, itself topped by a shallow dome oddly corrugated with alternate convex and concave ribs. Some of the capitals helping transfer the weight of the roof onto the columns are deeply incised with stylized plant motifs and the monogram of Justinian and Theodora can still be seen on a few. As it was converted into a **mosque** in the sixteenth century, nothing remains of its original mosaics, though a frieze inscribed with

Küçük Aya Sofya Camii

Greek letters honours Justinian, Theodora and St Sergius (the latter one of two **Christian martyrs**, both soldiers who later became patron saints of the Roman army, after whom the church was named). The proportions of the brick-built church have been spoiled by the addition, after its conversion to a mosque, of a five-domed "last prayer place" porch. Opposite the main door is a pleasant courtyard *medrese* with a teahouse.

Sokollu Mehmet Paşa Camii

MAP P.26, POCKET MAP G8
Mehmet Paşa Yokusu ⓜ 1 Sultanahmet.

Tricky to find in the narrow lanes a short walk uphill from the Church of St Sergius and Bacchus, this small mosque, designed by the brilliant **Sinan** and finished in 1571, is exquisite. The courtyard, very large in proportion to the prayer hall, has at its centre a pretty ablutions fountain. It is ringed on three sides by dome-topped colonnades, beneath which are ranged the cells of a still-active boys' Koran school. The intimate prayer hall is almost square and covered by a high dome supported by four semi-domes. This interior is a model of restraint, with the finest-period İznik tiles used, sparingly, to enliven the pale stonework. Soft light filters in through the coloured glass in the tracery-work windows, and worked into the lintel above the door and embedded in the *mimber* are pieces of stone said to be from the sacred Kaaba in **Mecca**. The mosque was built for Süleyman the Magnificent's last grand vizier, Sokollu Mehmet Paşa.

Museum of Turkish and Islamic Arts (Türk Ve Islam Eserleri Müzesi)

MAP P.26, POCKET MAP G12
Atmeydanı Sok 6 ⓜ 1 Sultanahmet ⓣ 0212 518 1805. Charge.

Sokullu Mehmet Paşa Camii

Located a little west of the Blue Mosque and flanking the Hippodrome, this impressive museum houses exhibits from the Islamic world including oriental **carpets**, illuminated Korans, calligraphy, Ottoman and Persian miniatures, tiles, ceramics, metalwork, intricately carved wooden doors and mother of pearl inlaid furniture, as well as ethnographical artefacts. The building is a former palace, originally home to İbrahim Paşa, grand vizier to the greatest Ottoman sultan, Süleyman the Magnificent. Completed in 1524, it was rebuilt following a devastating fire in 1843. İbrahim was the empire's most successful grand vizier and during his thirteen years in office he amassed enormous wealth. Eventually incurring the mistrust of Süleyman, the unfortunate statesman was strangled in the Topkapı Palace. Today, the museum is home to over **40,000 exhibits** dating from the earliest years of Islam in the late seventh century to today, though the main focus is on the Selçuk Turkish (eleventh to thirteenth centuries) and Ottoman

(fourteenth to nineteenth centuries) periods. The major exhibition room, once the Great Hall of the palace, houses stunning Turkish carpets ranging from threadbare thirteenth-century rugs to superbly preserved giants weighing thousands of kilograms that once graced the Topkapı Palace. In the basement, the fascinating ethnography section is home to a **black goat-hair tent** woven by the nomadic *Yörük* tribes of the Taurus Mountains, descendants of the Turkoman nomads who poured into Anatolia from the eleventh century onwards.

Hippodrome (Meydanı)
MAP P.26, POCKET MAP G11–12
🚊 1 Sultanahmet.

Set between the landmark Blue Mosque and the Museum of Turkish and Islamic Art, this paved, rectangular public park area was, in the Roman and Byzantine periods, a **stadium**. The original incarnation dates to 203 AD, when Emperor Septimius Severus rebuilt the city, but it was enlarged when Constantine made it the imperial capital in 330. Used during the Byzantine period for court

Egyptian obelisk at the Hippodrome at Meydani

ceremonies and games – most notably chariot racing – it was some 480m long and 117.5m wide and held up to 100,000 spectators. Spectacles in the Hippodrome were presided over by the emperor and his entourage from the *kathisma* or royal box, situated in the vicinity of what today forms the grounds of the Blue Mosque. At the northeast end of the Hippodrome, close to the tramway on Divan Yolu, is the attractive domed **Fountain of Kaiser Wilhelm II**, gifted to the then Ottoman sultan by the German leader in 1898 and located where the starting gates for the chariot races used to be. Southwest of this, following what was the central line or *spina* of the course, is the **Egyptian Obelisk**. Shipped here from Egypt in the fourth century, it is covered in hieroglyphic symbols and dates back to the sixteenth century BC. Intriguingly, it is mounted on a sandstone block carved on all four sides with images of Theodosius I, the emperor responsible for its erection, overseeing the chariot races from the royal box.

Continuing down the *spina* you'll find the **Serpentine Column**, comprising three intertwined bronze snakes, today sadly headless, though one is displayed in the city's Archeology Museum. Cast to celebrate a Greek victory over the invading Persians in 479 BC, it was brought here from Delphi by Constantine I. The last monument is a crude stone obelisk, the **Column of Constantine**, which also served as a race marker. Beyond this was a raised semicircular seating area lining the curved end of the course where the chariots turned. Known as the **sphendrome**, the seating has been subsumed by more modern buildings, but its massive substructure is visible from Nakilbent Sokak below. The course of the Hippodrome was used for state ceremonies in Ottoman times, hence its Turkish name **At Meydanı** or "square of the horses".

Blue Mosque (Sultanahmet Camii)

MAP P.26, POCKET MAP G12
Sultanahmet Meydanı ⓘ 1 Sultanahmet.
Closed to non-Muslims at prayer times and Friday mornings.

Properly known as the Sultanahmet Camii in Turkish, after the

Ottoman sultan Ahmet I who commissioned it, this is probably the single most visited sight in Istanbul. Completed in 1616 after seven years' labour, the mosque takes its more tourist-friendly name from the carapace of predominantly **blue İznik tiles** liberally adorning its interior. Along with the Haghia Sophia it dominates the skyline of Sultanahmet, its majestic flow of domes and half-domes encompassed by six slender, cylindrical minarets (the latter reviled by the pious at the time of construction for consciously imitating the Great Mosque in Mecca) quite breathtaking to behold – especially when atmospherically illuminated at night. The best approach is from the Hippodrome, where a splendid doorway leads into the *avlu* or courtyard, which covers virtually the same ground area as the prayer hall itself. Only Muslims can enter the prayer hall via the main, northwest-facing door; other visitors must exit the courtyard and enter via the southwest portal, where there are often long queues. Even though

non-Muslims are kept back from much of the prayer hall by a rope barrier, the cavernous interior, with its large **central dome**, 23.5m in diameter and 43m high, flanked by four smaller semi-domes and supported by four enormous ribbed columns, is impressive. The twenty thousand-plus İznik tiles vie with each other for the visitors' attention and the prayer wall at the southeast end is pierced by the standard Mecca-facing prayer niche, the *mihrab*. To the right is the *mimber* or pulpit, used by the imam to lead prayers. To the left the loge, a raised platform for the sultan and his entourage, is connected to a royal pavilion attached to the easternmost corner of the building. Only visible from outside, this contains a suite of rooms used by the sultan on days he visited, and was reached by a sloping ramp, allowing access by horse. **Sultan Ahmet I's tomb** (free), an attractively domed structure, stands in the northern corner of the grounds, accessible from Mimar Mehmet Ağa Caddesi. The sultan was buried here with his wife and three of his sons.

SULTANAHMET

Cistern of the 1001 Columns

Tram on Divan Yolu

Cistern of 1001 Columns

MAP P.26, POCKET MAP G11
İmran Öktem Cad ☺1 Sultanahmet ☎0212
518 1001. Charge.

Despite the fact that it has been
turned into a posh function space
for business meetings, gala events,
functions and weddings among
other things (when it is closed to
visitors), it's well worth having a
look inside this covered cistern,
another of the ones that were so
crucial to the growth of Byzantine
Constantinople. At around 64m
by 56m, it's not quite as large as
the much better known Basilica
Cistern, not far to the east along
Divan Yolu, but it is still the second
largest in the city. The pretty,
herring-bone-patterned brick
domes of the vault are supported by
224 columns erected in 16 rows of
14. The total height of the interior
is nearly 15m, though it is difficult
to get a true impression of this as
the false wooden floor, inserted
when it was converted into a
function space, is raised well above
the original ground level.

Divan Yolu

MAP P.26, POCKET MAP G11

☺1 Sultanahmet.

Just north of the Cistern of
1001 Columns is Divan Yolu,
today Sultanahmet's busiest
thoroughfare as, despite being
semi-pedestrianized (watch out for
speeding service vehicles), it carries
the incredibly useful T1 tramline.
In Roman and Byzantine times
it was the most important street
in the city. Then known as the
Mese or Middleway, it could be
followed from the Milion (see page
24) west out of the city and on
to the Adriatic. It became Divan
Yolu in the Ottoman period as it
led visitors and petitioners to the
Divan (council) chamber in the
Topkapı Palace.

On the south side of Divan
Yolu is the **Firuz Ağa Camii**,
one of the city's earliest mosques.
Built in 1491, compared to the
nearby Blue Mosque it is a model
of architectural restraint, being
little more than a square prayer
hall surmounted by a dome
attended by a single minaret. It
is well used by the local faithful,
and like all mosques in the city
has (useful for visitors) public
toilets attached.

Shops

Chez Galip

MAP P.26, POCKET MAP G12

At Meydanı 78 ⓘ 1 Sultanahmet
Ⓦ chezgalip.com.

Sells pottery crafted in the central Anatolian pottery town of Avanos, the most intriguing of which are those based on ancient Hittite designs. There is plenty of decent quality İznik pottery on show too.

Cocoon

MAP P.26, POCKET MAP G9

Küçük Aya Sofya Cad 13 ⓘ 1 Sultanahmet
ⓘ 0212 638 6450.

A positive cornucopia of richly hued artefacts made from felt – bags, hats, figurines and the like, plus an array of carpets, kilims and throws from Central Asia.

Galeri Kayseri

MAP P.26, POCKET MAP G11

Divan Yolu 58 ⓘ 1 Sultanahmet
Ⓦ galerikayseri.com.

The best bookshop in the old city, this is the place to come if you want a specialist book on İstanbul – though prices are considerably higher than at home. There's another branch diagonally opposite, and both stock English-language novels.

İznik Classics

MAP P.26, POCKET MAP H12

Arasta Çarşısı ⓘ 1 Sultanahmet,
Ⓦ iznikclassics.com.

İznik ceramics were, at their best, among the finest wares produced in the Ottoman Empire. The gorgeous tiles sold here today are handcrafted in the same traditional way by studio potters – and are very expensive as a result.

Jennifer's Hamam

MAP P.26, POCKET MAP H12

Arasta Çarşısı ⓘ 1 Sultanahmet
Ⓦ www.jennifershamam.com.

Run by a friendly Canadian, the big draw here is that all the textiles for sale are hand-woven from organic cotton, linen or silk. Choose from a bewildering array of all-cotton *peştemals*, Turkish bath wraps (widely popular for use as lightweight beach towels), high quality, traditional fluffy towels and a dazzling selection of colourful scarves.

Yörük Collection

MAP P.26, POCKET MAP G10

Yerebatan Cad 35 ⓘ 1 Sultanahmet
Ⓦ yoruk.com.

A well-laid-out shop that tries, and mostly succeeds, in being all things to all people, with all manner of traditional (and modern interpretations of) Turkish handicrafts, from carpets to silver jewellery and Ottoman miniatures to cushion covers.

Cafés

Çiğdem Patisserie

MAP P.26, POCKET MAP G11

Divan Yolu Cad 62 ⓘ 1 Sultanahmet
Ⓦ cigdempastanesi.com.

Babouches

Çiğdem Patisserie

This busy, continental-style patisserie is as popular with locals as visitors. Temptingly arrayed in the window are savoury snacks such as *poğaça*, soft bread rolls stuffed with cheese or a slightly spiced potato mixture; semi-sweet *tahinli ekmek*, a bread spiral coated in sweetened sesame paste; and a huge range of sweets ranging from nut-stuffed *baklava* to *acıbadem*, Turkey's monster-sized answer to Italy's Amaretto biscuit. Black tea is served good and hot in tulip-shaped glasses, and there's a decent range of coffees, from Turkish-style to a very palatable latte. €

Edebiyat Kiraathanesi

MAP P.26, POCKET MAP G11
Divan Yolu Cad 14 ⓘ 1 Sultanahmet
ⓣ 0212 514 9068.
Elegant period tearooms right next to the Sultanahmet tram stop, with a superb range of Turkish desserts, coffees from Turkish to latte and glasses of tea. It's run by the Turkish Society for Literature,

so expect cultured Turks at the next table. €

The Pudding Shop

MAP P.26, POCKET MAP G11
Divan Yolu Cad 6 ⓘ 1 Sultanahmet
ⓦ puddingshop.com.
The service is canteen-style, the queues can be long and the food OK rather than exceptional, but this bustling café played a signature role in the hippy era as "the" hangout for travellers heading to India. The same owners still run it today, and continue serving the *sütlaç* (rice pudding) from which its unofficial name derives (it's more properly the *Lale Restaurant*). It also does a wide range of traditional savoury dishes, with mains such as *köfte* (meatballs), kebabs and stews – and is licensed. €

Tarihi Sultanahmet Köftecisi

MAP P.26, POCKET MAP G11
Divan Yolu Cad 4 ⓘ 1 Sultanahmet.

If you don't like grilled meatballs don't even consider this place. If you do, it is an Istanbul institution and one of the few places in tourist-orientated Sultanahmet to attract large numbers of Turkish diners. The owners are proud of the myriad Turkish celebrities who have eaten here, their photos and letters of thanks adorning the walls. What you get is firm *köfte* (meatballs) accompanied by a white bean salad, spicy tomato sauce, pickled peppers and crusty bread – best chased down with the salty yoghurt drink *ayran*. Unlicensed. €€

Restaurants

Albura Kathisma

MAP P.26, POCKET MAP H12
Akbıyık Cad 26 ☉ 1 Sultanahmet
ⓦ alburakathisma.com.

One of the best options on this bustling hotel-, restaurant- and bar-lined street, with an attractive bare-brick interior and tables outside. Service is good by Turkish standards and the wine (go for a recognized brand like Angora) reasonably priced. Meze include *mücver*, courgette fritters, served here in garlicky yoghurt. Traditional Anatolian dishes are the real pull, though, usually lamb or chicken based – try the lamb casserole with figs and almonds. Licensed. €€

Amedros

MAP P.26, POCKET MAP G11
Hoca Rüstem Paşa Sok 7 ☉ 1 Sultanahmet
ⓦ amedroscafe.com.

Tucked-away up a pedestrian alleyway off Divan Yolu, this professionally run place successfully combines local and international cuisine. The subtly lit interior is effortlessly stylish, all bare boards and neutral walls, though in summer the most popular tables are those out in the alleyway. The mixed-meze plate is very popular, with seven types of Turkish starters.

Mains include traditional dishes such as Ottoman chicken served in a sweet-sour sauce with rice. Licensed. Reservations advised. €€€

Balıkçı Sabahattin

MAP P.26, POCKET MAP H12
Seyit Hasan Kuyu Sok 1 ☉ 1 Sultanahmet
or ☉ 1 Cankurtaran ☏ 0212 458 1824.

Unpromisingly located – or set in a charmingly dilapidated area of town down by the defunct railway line – whatever your view, it can't be denied that this is the only Sultanahmet-area restaurant to draw monied locals from elsewhere in the city. The attraction here is freshly caught and cooked fish – from bluefish to sea bass, swordfish to red mullet – enjoyed in winter in an atmospheric old wooden house or, in summer, on tables set out front on a vine-shaded cobbled area. It's expensive, but you are paying to eat alongside Istanbul's elite. Licensed. Reservations advised. €€€€

Doy Doy

MAP P.26, POCKET MAP G12
Sifa Hama Sok 13 ☉ 1 Sultanahmet ☏ 0212 517 1588.

Balıkçı Sabahattin

This four-storey restaurant serves local workers and the more impecunious visitor, concentrating on hearty portions of Turkish standards. There's *pide* (Turkish pizza, big ovals of semi-leavened *pide* bread topped by cheese or meat), plenty of kebabs, classic soups such as *mercimek çorbası* (lentil soup) and, definitely best at lunchtime, *sulu yemek* (various stews served-up from steamtrays). Unlicensed. €€

Dubb

MAP P.26, POCKET MAP H11
Incili Çavuş Sok ① 1 Sultanahmet
Ⓦ dubbindian.com.

Indian restaurants are as rare as hens' teeth in Istanbul, so to find one so good in Sultanahmet is quite something. There are a few tables set out on the quiet street, otherwise dining is in a series of small rooms spread over four floors or, with fantastic views, a roof terrace. Tandoori dishes are the speciality, though there are thalis and fish dishes. Licensed. Reservations advised. €€

Matbah's terrace

Giritli

MAP P.26, POCKET MAP H9
Kerestici Hakkı Sok ① 1 Sultanahmet or
① 1 Cankurtaran ① 0212 458 2270.

The main reason to come here, and it's a worthy one, is to enjoy a full-blown set menu, which includes all (local) alcoholic drinks, over twenty mini-meze, three hot starters, a grilled fish main, and fruit to follow. The food, based on traditional Cretan recipes, is very good quality and the dining room is in a period wooden house, with a shady garden just across the street for alfresco summer eating. This is a good place to try *rakı*, the traditional aniseed spirit, a wonderful accompaniment to fish. Reservations advised. €€€

Matbah

MAP P.26, POCKET MAP H11
Caferiye Sok 6/1 ① 1 Sultanahmet
Ⓦ matbahrestaurant.com.

This concept restaurant, attached to the *Ottoman Imperial Hotel*, bases all its dishes on those once prepared in the kitchens of the Topkapı Palace. Ottoman cuisine, much richer than standard contemporary Turkish cooking, used fruit in many recipes. Try *kavun dolması*, melon stuffed with lamb and pilaf rice, or *mahmudiye*, tender cinnamon-flavoured chicken served with almonds and apricots. White-clothed tables are laid out on a plant-decked terrace overlooking the leaded domes of the Cafer Ağa Theological School. Licensed. Reservations advised. €€€

Şirvan Sofrasi

MAP P.26, POCKET MAP G9
Küçük Ayasofya Cad 71 ① 1 Sultanahmet
Ⓦ www.sirvan-sofrasi.com.

This restaurant of Ottoman cuisine available at reasonable prices The food is well presented and both locals and tourists. a water pipe (*nargile*) on the terrace. €€

Pierre Loti Roof-Bar

Bars

Cozy Pub

MAP P.26, POCKET MAP G11
Divan Yolu Cad 66 ⊕ 1 Sultanahmet
Ⓦ facebook.com/cozypubrestaurant.
Probably the most atmospheric bar
in Sultanahmet, with a pub-like
dark wood interior and plenty
of tables in the narrow alley
disgorging onto Divan Yolu. The
beers are a tad more expensive
than usual, but worth it for the
ambience. It also does quite
reasonable international/Turkish
food, including usual suspects like
pasta, burgers and salads.

Istanbul Terrace Bar

MAP P.26, POCKET MAP G11
Dr Imran Oktem Cad 1 ⊕ 1 Sultanahmet
⊕ 0212 516 9696.
The terrace bar of the *Arcadia Blue
Hotel* gives one of the best vantage
points in the city. To the southeast
the Sea of Marmara glimmers
behind the Hippodrome and Blue
Mosque, straight ahead the Haghia
Sophia and grounds of the Topkapı
Palace are backed by distant Asia,
and to the northeast stretches the
thin ribbon of the Bosphorus. It

all looks particularly appealing,
conveniently enough for those in
need of a drink at the end of a day's
exploration, as the sun goes down.

Just Bar

MAP P.26, POCKET MAP H12
Akbıyık Cad 28 ⊕ 0532 387 5729.
This lively bar is very popular
with guests from the myriad
hotels and hostels in this popular
neighbourhood. There's a small
seating area fronting the busy
street, perfect for people-watching
on warm evenings, and inside the
tables are cleared to make a small
dancefloor on weekend nights.

Pierre Loti Roof-Bar

MAP P.26, POCKET MAP G8
Piyer Loti Cad 5 ⊕ 1 Sultanahmet ⊕ 0212
518 5700.
Hotel bars seldom drip character
and this place, though smart,
is no exception. But the vistas
over Istanbul's exotic skyline are
fabulous – best enjoyed at sunset.
It's quite pricey, but your drink
comes accompanied by a bowl
of quality *çerez* (salted Turkish
nibbles that usually include roasted
chickpeas, peanuts, almonds and
pistachios).

Topkapı Palace to the Golden Horn

Superbly located on the first of the old city's seven hills, right at the snout of the peninsula pointing up the continent-dividing Bosphorus strait, the Topkapı Palace was the nerve centre of the powerful Ottoman Empire. This sprawling, walled compound encompasses not only the courtyards and pavilions of the palace itself but also Istanbul's excellent Archeology Museum, an important Byzantine church and Gülhane Park, the only major green and open space in the congested old city. Following the busy tramline downhill to the northwest, you come to the more workaday business district of Sirkeci, best known to visitors for its late nineteenth-century station, once the easternmost terminus of the famous Orient Express. Beyond it, fronting the ferry-filled waters of the Golden Horn, is mega-bustling Eminönü, with its fragrant, Ottoman-era Spice Bazaar.

Archeology Museum (Arkeoloji Müzesi)

MAP P.44, POCKET MAP H7

Osman Hamdi Bey Yokuşu ⓘ 1 Gülhane Ⓦ muze.gov.tr. Charge, extra for audio guide.

Reached either from the first court of the Topkapı Palace or via the main entrance to Gülhane Park, this fascinating but often overlooked museum comprises three separate sections, each housed in a historic building. The first, on your left as you enter, is the small **Museum of the Ancient Orient**, built in 1883. Pick of the exhibits is a clay tablet inscribed in cuneiform, copied from a silver original, marking a treaty signed between the Hittites and Egyptians after a major battle in 1269 BC. This was the world's first known peace treaty, and a copy is housed in the UN headquarters in New York. The blue and yellow glazed bricks, decorated with animals in raised relief and dating to the reign of Nebuchadnezzar (604–562 BC), once formed a frieze lining the processional way to Babylon's Ishtar Gate. The monumental Neoclassical-style building on the right as you head into the grounds was built by French architect Vallaury in 1891. This is the main building of the **Archeology Museum** complex, and contains a stunning array of artefacts ranging from the Paleolithic to the Ottoman periods. Unmissable, on the ground floor, are the **Sidon Sarcophagi**, discovered in the late nineteenth century in what is today, Lebanon. The relief-carving on the surfaces of the Alexander, Lycian and Mourning Women sarcophagi is quite superb. These sarcophagi are merely the best of hundreds more displayed in rooms to the left of the Sidon Sarcophagi. Also on the ground floor is a comprehensive display of marble statuary, arranged chronologically and spanning the Archaic to

Roman periods. The whole collection of statuary is superbly lit and presented. Upstairs is an equally impressive array of well-presented archeological treasures, many from the 'legendary' city of Troy on Turkey's northwest Aegean coast. Opposite the main building is the third museum in the complex, the **Museum of Turkish Ceramics**. Built in the fifteenth century as part of the Topkapı Palace complex and known as the Çinili Köşk or Tiled Pavilion, it houses a vibrant display of Turkish tiles and other ceramic wares.

Haghia Eirene (Aya İrini)

MAP P.44, POCKET MAP H7
Charge.

The predominantly brick-built Haghia Eirene or "Church of the Holy Peace", is tucked away in the northwest corner of the first court of the Topkapı Palace. One of the earliest churches in Constantinople, it burned down in the same 532 riot that destroyed the second incarnation of the Haghia Sophia (see page 25) and was rebuilt in its current form soon after. It is rectangular in shape and topped by

Haghia Eirene

a relatively small dome surmounted on a drum. Inside, the most prominent features are the simple black on gold mosaic cross in the apse and, below it, a curved seating area for the clergy, the synthronon.

Topkapı Palace (Topkapı Sarayı)

MAP P.44, POCKET MAP J7
Topkapı Sarayı Müzesi ⊙ 1 Sultanahmet
ⓦ muze.gen.tr. Charge, extra for audio guide.

Completed in 1465, this palace complex, a collection of buildings ranged around four large courtyards, was the administrative and political heart of the Ottoman Empire until 1853, when the sultan decamped to the European-style Dolmabahçe Palace across the Golden Horn. Along with neighbours the Haghia Sophia and Blue Mosque, it's the most visited sight in Istanbul. Enter the **first court** (free admission) by the Bab-ı-Hümayün, a gateway piercing the defensive wall which separated the palace from the city. This area was home to the bakeries and imperial mint. The ticket office for the remainder of

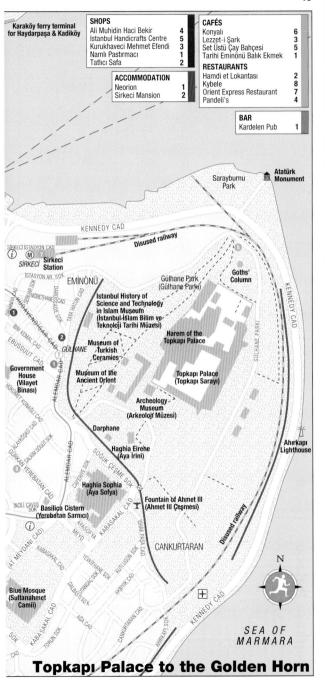

SHOPS	
Ali Muhidin Haci Bekir	4
Istanbul Handicrafts Centre	5
Kurukhaveci Mehmet Efendi	3
Namlı Pastırmacı	1
Tatlıcı Safa	2

CAFÉS	
Konyalı	6
Lezzet-i Şark	3
Set Üstü Çay Bahçesi	5
Tarihi Eminönü Balık Ekmek	1

ACCOMMODATION	
Neorion	1
Sirkeci Mansion	2

RESTAURANTS	
Hamdi et Lokantası	2
Kybele	8
Orient Express Restaurant	7
Pandeli's	4

BAR	
Kardelen Pub	1

Karaköy ferry terminal for Haydarpaşa & Kadiköy

Sarayburnu Park

Atatürk Monument

KENNEDY CAD

Disused railway

SIRKECI İSTASYON CAD

SİRKECİ Sirkeci Station

İSTASYON AR. SOK

EMİNÖNÜ

Gülhane Park (Gülhane Parkı)

Goths' Column

KENNEDY CAD

NÖBETHANE CAD

DARÜSSADE CAD

TAYA HATUN CAD

Istanbul History of Science and Technology in Islam Museum (İstanbul İslam Bilim ve Teknoloji Tarihi Müzesi)

GÜLHANE PARKI

İBNİ KEMAL CAD

EBUSSUUT CAD

GÜLHANE

Museum of Turkish Ceramics

Harem of the Topkapı Palace

Government House (Vilayet Binası)

Museum of the Ancient Orient

Topkapı Palace (Topkapı Sarayı)

HÜKÜMET KONAĞI CAD

ALEMDAR CAD

Archeology Museum (Arkeoloji Müzesi)

Ahırkapı Lighthouse

ALAYKÖŞKÜ CAD

GÜRKAN YEREBATAN CAD

SALKIM SÖĞÜT SOK

Darphane

SOĞUK ÇEŞME SOK

Haghia Eirehe (Aya İrini)

CEBİRYE SOK

Haghia Sophia (Aya Sofya)

INCILI ÇAVUŞ SOK

Basilica Cistern (Yerebatan Sarnıcı)

Fountain of Ahmet III (Ahmet III Çeşmesi)

AYASOFYA

KABASAKAL SOK

İŞHAK PAŞA CAD

Disused railway

(AT MEYDANI CADI)

KABASAKAL SOK

KABASAKAL MEYDI

CANKURTARAN

TEVKİFHANE SOK

KUTLUGÜN SOK

N

Blue Mosque (Sultanahmet Camii)

DALBASTI SOK

AKBIYIK CAD

AKBIYIK CAD

KABA SAKAL CAD

TORUN SOK

AĞA CAD

CANKURTARAN CAD

KENNEDY CAD

AHIRKAPI SOK

SEA OF MARMARA

Topkapı Palace to the Golden Horn

Topkapı Palace

1 Ortakapı or Middle Gate
2 Kitchens and Cooks' Quarters
3 Stables and Harness Rooms
4 Barrack of the Halberdiers of the Long Tresses
5 Hall of the Divan
6 Offices of the Divan
7 Inner Treasury
8 Gate of Felicity (Bab-üs Saadet)
9 Throne Room
10 Library of Sultanahmet III
11 Rooms of the Relics of the Prophet
12 Imperial Treasury (Pavilion of Mehmet II)
13 Hall of the Expeditionary Force
14 Circumcision Köşkü
15 Baghdad Köşkü
16 Revan Köşkü
17 Tulip Gardens of Ahmet III
18 Mustafa Paşa Köşkü
19 Mecidiye Köşkü
20 Entry to the Harem (Carriage Gate)
21 Aviary Gate (Kuşhane Kapısı)
22 Valide Sultan's Court
23 Valide Sultan's Dining Room
24 Valide Sultan's Bedroom
25 Golden Road
26 Ahmet III Dining Room

the courts is in the wall to the right of the Bab-ı Selam or **Gate of Salutations**, with its fairy-tale-like conical turrets. Inside the gate are a couple of models of the palace complex, useful for orientation. The **second court** is flanked to the right by the kitchens, to the left are the Privy Stables and the Divan. The latter, beautifully decorated in sixteenth-century Ottoman style, was the council chamber where the chief officials (viziers) met to discuss matters of state, secretly watched from a grilled window in the wall behind by the sultan. Next door, the inner treasury is now the **Armoury Museum**. Court ceremonies were presided over, and military campaigns launched, by the sultan seated on his throne in front of the Babüs Saadet or **Gate of Felicity**. Beyond this, the **third court** was the nerve centre of the Ottoman-era palace as it contained both the Palace School, which trained the empire's officials, as well as the **Throne Room** where decisions taken in the Divan were sealed by the sultan. Behind the Throne Room is the pretty **Library of Sultanahmet**

III. The **Rooms of the Relics of the Prophet** in the northwest corner of the court contain the mantle and standard of the Prophet Mohammed, among many other holy relics, while the **Imperial Treasury** to the right is now home to treasures amassed by the sultans over the centuries, including the famed Topkapı Dagger and Spoonmaker's Diamond. The **Hall of the Expeditionary Force**, in the same row as the treasury, contains some splendid costumes worn by various sultans. The fourth court was devoted to leisure, comprising a series of **pavilions** set in pretty gardens, including the Baghdad, Revan and Circumcision pavilions. There are fine views across the Bosphorus to Asia from the Mecidiye Pavilion.

Harem of the Topkapı Palace

MAP P.44, POCKET MAP H6
Topkapı Palace, second court ❶ 1 Sultanahmet. Charge.

Owing to its location within the grounds of the Topkapı Palace's second court, you can't visit the **women's quarters,** or Harem

Circumcision Room (Topkapı Palace)

(literally meaning "forbidden" in Arabic), without first paying to enter the palace itself. The Harem was a suite of rooms within the palace complex, over four hundred of them, where the sultan's wives, female slaves (concubines) and children resided. It also contained the quarters of the Black Eunuchs who guarded them, and the private quarters of the sultan. Largely constructed during the reign of Murat III in the late sixteenth century, the Harem is thus a century or so more recent than the Topkapı Palace. The ticket office is by the distinctive Divan Tower, entry through the **Carriage Gate**, so called because this is where the concubines mounted carriages for trips out. Leading right through the maze-like complex, from its entrance in the second court to its exit in the third, is a cobbled path known as the Golden Way, purportedly named after a new sultan's habit of throwing gold coins to his concubines. The first important suite of rooms are those of the **Valide Sultan** (the sultan's mother), ranged around a spacious courtyard. North of here are the

apartments and reception rooms of the sultan himself. Largest is the **Imperial Hall**, lush with Baroque gilt and İznik tiles, where the sultan entertained visitors. More beautiful though is **Murat III's Salon**, designed by Sinan in 1578 and boasting a stunning bronze fireplace and walls gleaming with finest-period İznik tiles. The small, domed **Library of Ahmet I** (1608–09) is exquisite, as is the **dining room of Ahmet III**, probably so called because of the bowls of fruit painted on the wood-panelled walls. The notorious Cage, where the sultan's brothers were confined to avoid squabbles between potential successors to the throne, was probably located in rooms on the first floor, closed to visitors. Exit the complex through the **Aviary Gate**.

Gülhane Park (Gülhane Parki)

MAP P.44, POCKET MAP H6
Alemdar Cad ⓘ 1 Gülhane.

Once the extended gardens of the Topkapı Palace, today Gülhane Park makes a great place to escape the tourist bustle of the big-hitter

Gülhane Park

İznik tiles

Both the Topkapı Palace and its Harem gleam with them, as does the Rüstem Paşa Camii, the Sokollu Mehmet Paşa Camii and scores of Ottoman-era buildings across the city. The Blue Mosque even derives its "English" name from the predominantly blue İznik tiles sheathing its interior. Production began in İznik (ancient Nicea) on the south shores of the Sea of Marmara in the fifteenth century and soon these tiles, inspired by Persian designs and made mostly from quartz rather than clay, became all the rage. So much so that by the sixteenth century there were over three hundred kilns churning out top-quality tiles (and other ceramics), often decorated with blue stylized flowers or geometric shapes on a white ground, enlivened by splashes of vivid red. Quality and output peaked in the late sixteenth and early seventeenth centuries. After a long period of decline, studio-potters based in İznik have revived the art.

sights on the crown of the hill above. A few pieces of distinctly average play equipment for young kids aside, there's little to do except unwind, though it's worth strolling down to the **Goths' Column** in the northeast of the park, not far from the tip of the peninsula at Saray Burnu (Palace Point). Built to commemorate a third- or fourth-century victory over said Goths, it is over 18m high and topped by a large, intricately carved Corinthian capital. Nearby is *Set Üstü Çay Bahçesi* (see page 56), a decent tea garden with great views up the Bosphorus and across to Asia.

Istanbul History of Science and Technology in Islam Museum (İstanbul İslam Bilim ve Teknoloji Tarihi Müzesi)

MAP P.44, POCKET MAP H6
Gülhane Parkı 🚇 1 Gülhane 🕿 0212 528 8065. Charge.

Showcasing the invaluable contribution made to civilization by scientists and inventors from the Islamic world between the eighth and sixteenth centuries, this museum is housed in what were the imperial stables, built into the inside of the walls encircling Gülhane Park. If you're looking for genuine artefacts, be prepared to be disappointed, as all the exhibits are meticulous models made at Johann Wolfgang von Goethe University, Frankfurt. The replicas are impressive, however, and are beautifully displayed artworks in their own right, not least an elephant-shaped water clock based on a twelfth-century original, and a planetarium based on an idea by tenth-century astronomer as-Sigzi.

Cağaloğlu Hamamı

MAP P.44, POCKET MAP G6
Kazım İsmail Gürkan Cad 34 🚇 1 Sultanahmet 🌐 cagalogluhamami.com.tr. Charge.

Some 400m north of Divan Yolu, these **Turkish baths** are probably the most famous in the city, not least because *Indiana Jones and the Temple of Doom* included a scene shot in this hamam, and luminaries as varied as Florence Nightingale and John Travolta are reputed to have bathed here. It was built in 1741 during the reign of Sultan Mahmut I in Ottoman Baroque style, and its profits were used to fund the sultan's library in the Aya Sofya Camii. In an era when only the very richest citizens had private baths, establishments such as these were essential for both cleanliness and hygiene and not, as they are today, merely an (admittedly thoroughly pleasurable) afterthought to a day's sightseeing. Bathers begin in the *camekan*, the largest room in the bathhouse, surmounted by a large dome, where there are changing rooms and areas to relax with tea or other refreshments. Beyond the small *soğukluk* or cold room is the main event, the *hararet* or steam room, presided over by a large dome supported by a circle of columns, which diffuses soft light through the tiny, round glass windows studding it. The bathhouse comprises two sections, with separate entrances and bathing rooms for men and women.

Alemdar Street (Alemdar Caddesi)

MAP P.44, POCKET MAP H7

🚇 1 Gülhane.

The lower part of this street, from where it curves around past the main entrance to Gülhane Park, has a few points of interest up and down it when crossing. The first, actually just above the park entrance, is the **Zeynep**

The marble kiosk on Alemdar Caddesi

Sultan Camii. At first sight this attractive building looks very much like a Byzantine church, with its contrasting bands of brick and pale-coloured stone and scallop-edged dome. It is in fact a mosque, built in 1769 by Zeynep, daughter of Sultan Ahmet III. Not far below it is a small, domed and extremely pretty **marble kiosk** (*büfe* in Turkish) selling cigarettes, gum, tissues and the like. In the Ottoman period this was a *sebil*, from which free water was handed out to passers-by. These *sebil*s were dotted throughout the city, donated by wealthy citizens who hoped to secure their place in paradise through their good deeds. A short way down the street is a grand gateway on the left, notable for its sinuous, Baroque-style overhanging roof – the **Bab-ı Ali** – remodelled in 1843. From the mid-eighteenth century onwards, this gate led to the personal quarters and offices of the grand vizier, the chief official of the Ottoman Empire, where most state business was handled – an institution which became known to the West as the Sublime Porte. Opposite is the **Alay Köşk**, built into the line of walls now surrounding the park but which were originally the outer fortifications of the Topkapı Palace, built in 1465 by Mehmet the Conqueror. Beautifully restored in 2011, this polygonal structure allowed suspicious sultans to observe the comings and goings of the Sublime Porte opposite. The more trusting used it to review the great processions held in the city, such as that of the Guilds, involving virtually every tradesman in the city and held every fifty years or so. Deli İbrahim, or İbrahim the Mad (1640–48), is reputed to have shot passers-by with a crossbow from this eyrie. Access is from inside the park, with a sloping ramp allowing the sultan to enter without dismounting.

Men getting massages in Cağaloğlu Hamamı

Sirkeci Station

MAP P.44, POCKET MAP G6
Ankara Cad ⊙ 1 Sirkeci.

The eastern terminus of the fabled Orient Express, which first terminated here in 1888 after its 2900km journey from Paris via Vienna, Sirkeci Station has withstood the vicissitudes of time remarkably well. Intact are its clock towers, Moorish arches and Parisian-style domed roof, a surprisingly successful architectural hotchpotch of Neoclassical and Islamic architecture, designed by the Prussian architect August Jachmund. Many distinguished visitors once arrived at Sirkeci Station from Europe, including King Boris III of Bulgaria and Agatha Christie, the latter immortalizing the service in *Murder on the Orient Express*. Today, the station serves neither kings nor famous authors, or indeed overground trains. But inside this iconic station building is the Sirkeci stop on the Marmaray metro line (see page 147) which connects Europe to Asia via the Bosphorus tunnel.

There's also a small museum (free) for rail buffs (see page 147).

Central Sirkeci

MAP P.44, POCKET MAP G6
Sirkeci Merkez ⊙ 1 Sirkeci.

The heart of this bustling commercial district, centred on two major streets, Büyük Postane Caddesi and Hamidiye Caddesi, offers some early twentieth-century delights. Built in 1909 and easiest to find is the monumental **PTT Merkez** or **Central Post Office** on Büyük Postane Caddesi. It was designed by Paris-trained Turk Vedat Tak, an exponent of the First National Architectural Movement, which sought to blend Ottoman and western styles to produce original buildings representative of the rapidly modernizing empire. With its imposing stone facade combining Ottoman elements such as İznik tiles with Neoclassical Corinthian pilasters, it certainly succeeds. The inside of the building, with its glazed roof and period fittings, is worth a look even if you're not buying stamps. Diagonally opposite the PTT Merkez is an overtly European-style import, the Art Nouveau **Vlora Han**, today a run-down office block which nonetheless still impresses with its curved facade, panels of stylized roses in raised-relief plasterwork and whiplash wrought-iron balcony rails. Far more austere is the **Vakıf Han** on Hamidiye Caddesi. Built as a seven-storey office block to a design by another principal exponent of the First National Architectural Movement, Kemaleddin Bey, its severe stone facade, leavened by Ottoman-style domed turrets, conceals a steel skeleton.

Spice Bazaar (Mısır Çarşısı)

MAP P.44, POCKET MAP F6
Cami Meydanı ⓘ 1 Eminönü.
ⓦ misircarsisi.org.tr.

Close to the waterfront in Eminönü, the Spice Bazaar (*Mısır Çarşısı*) was built as part of the Yeni Cami complex, the revenues raised from it used to fund the running of the mosque and its associated philanthropic institutions. The L-shaped building is typically Ottoman in style, with 88 vaulted chambers and more rooms above,

usually entered by a monumental gateway at the northeast corner. The origins of its name are uncertain. *Mısır* in Turkish can mean either corn or Egypt, and it's possible this name derives either from the fact that in the Byzantine period the area was the centre of corn trading or that many of the spices imported into Istanbul came from Egypt. Today, the bazaar still sells myriad spices, usually attractively piled in mounds of contrasting colours (and smells) outside the hole-in-the-wall cells within, alongside other tempting goodies like Turkish delight and pistachio nuts. Prices are high, however, as this is the most popular market in the city after the Grand Bazaar, so look as the locals do in the surrounding streets for cheaper buys.

Around the Spice Bazaar

MAP P.44, POCKET MAP F6
ⓘ 1 Eminönü.

Keen shoppers should peruse **Tahmis Caddesi**, a row of stalls lining the western wall of the bazaar selling a huge variety of traditional Turkish cheeses, olives, nuts and spices as well as cured

Spice Bazaar

Among the bazaar stalls of Hasırcılar Caddesi

meats. There's more of the same on narrow **Hasırcılar Caddesi** (Street of the Strawmakers) running northwest of the bazaar. On the corner of Tahmis and Hasırcılar streets is the ever-busy coffee emporium *Kurukhaveci Mehmet Efendi* (see page 55), in one of Istanbul's few Art Deco buildings.

On the east side of the Spice Bazaar is a fascinating market, the **garden and pet bazaar**, which sells everything from caged goldfinches to chicks dyed the colours of the city's big football teams (a yellow chick and a red one would be for Galatasaray, a yellow and a blue for Fenerbahçe). You might even spot a leech wriggling in a jar.

Yeni Cami

MAP P.44, POCKET MAP G6
Yeni Cami Cad ⊕ 1 Eminönü.
The domes and minarets of the "New Mosque" soon become a familiar landmark to visitors heading up or across the Bosphorus, or trundling over the Galata Bridge to Galata/Beyoğlu on the north side of the Golden Horn, and the steps outside it are invariably busy, not least with

purveyors of seed to feed the thousands of pigeons that flock into the square in front of it. This was the last of the imperial mosques to be built in the city, hence its name, and although construction began in 1597, it wasn't completed until 1663. Like its predecessors, it was part of a complex to provide for the needs of the local community, comprising a hospital, soup kitchen, baths and fountains and, of course, the Spice Bazaar. Designed by an apprentice of the Ottoman Empire's master architect Sinan, the mosque follows convention, with the faithful first entering a large courtyard centred on a ritual ablutions fountain and surrounded on three sides by porticoes. The prayer hall, fronted by a raised platform covered by a portico for late comers or when the interior is packed, is cruciform in plan, the central dome flanked by four semi-domes.

Galata Bridge

MAP P.44, POCKET MAP F5
Eminönü ⊕ 1 Eminönü or Karaköy.
The entire Eminönü waterfront heaves with humanity: kindly souls

feeding pigeons in the square; the faithful heading to prayers in the Yeni Cami; commuters rushing to catch a ferry home to Asia, having elbowed their way to the best buys in the packed, narrow alleys around the Spice Bazaar; vendors flogging knock-off wares in one of the underpasses; and hungry visitors munching on cut-price fish sandwiches on the quay. So it's little surprise that the **Galata Bridge**, while far from being the most elegant or historic bridge in the world, is one of its busiest and most vibrant, accommodating as it does the overspill from the congested waterfront area. The lower deck is lined with cafés and restaurants, while the upper deck teems with anglers and itinerants peddling fake Adidas socks and gimcrack watches, shouting to be heard above the roar of trucks and rumble of the tram. The first bridge, built of wood in 1845, was some 500m long and symbolically linked the Muslim-dominated old city with the Christianized European quarters of Galata and Pera (Beyoğlu). Today's steel version dates back to the 1980s, and the central section can be hoisted to allow big ships access to the Golden Horn.

Rüstem Paşa Camii

MAP P.44, POCKET MAP F5
Hasırcılar Çarşısı ⓘ 1 Eminönü.

Dating back to 1561, internally this is one of the most attractive mosques in the whole of Istanbul. Another Sinan masterpiece, it is cleverly constructed on a raised terrace above the level of the alleys below. Built for Rüstem Paşa, the grand vizier of Süleyman the Magnificent in 1561, the mosque is reached by steps leading through a passageway to the terrace, which is dominated by an unusual double portico. The entrance for visitors is through a side-door to the left of the building. Essentially a simple dome supported by four large piers, its real wonder is the finest-period İznik tiles covering virtually every available surface. As usual, predominantly blue on a white ground, many of these tiles are embellished by the addition of vivid red, slightly raised-relief details. As this colour was very tricky for the craftsman to achieve, they represent the high point of İznik tile production.

Fishermen on Galata Bridge

Shops

Ali Muhidin Haci Bekir

MAP P.44, POCKET MAP G6
Hamidiye Cad 83 ⊙ 1 Eminönü ☎ 0216 379 4921.

This is not the cheapest place to buy traditional *lokum* (Turkish delight) but it is one of the best. Established way back in 1717, this charming shop stocks twenty-plus flavours of the sticky stuff, all colourfully displayed in a shop interior lined with old-fashioned wood shelves and glass-fronted cabinets. There's much more than *lokum* here too, including traditional boiled sweets, hazelnut-paste goodies and sugared almonds.

Istanbul Handicrafts Centre

MAP P.44, POCKET MAP G7
Nuruosmaniye Cd 32 ⊙ 1 Sultanahmet.
Housed in a restored *medrese* (Islamic theological school), this centre keeps alive traditional crafts such as bookbinding, marbling and calligraphy. It's worth visiting to see the building and the artisans at work, even if you choose not to purchase anything.

Kurukhaveci Mehmet Efendi

MAP P.44, POCKET MAP F5
Tahmis Sok 66 ⊙ 1 Eminönü ⓦ mehmetefendi.com.
An Istanbul institution, this is the place to come if you want to buy coffee roasted and ground the way it should be to make both genuine Turkish and filter coffee. The queues of locals from across the city attest to its quality. This Art Deco period gem of a shop also sells *sahlep*, a powdered orchid-root-based beverage popular in Istanbul's cold winters.

Namlı Pastırmacı

MAP P.44, POCKET MAP F5
Hasırcılar Cad 14 ⊙ 1 Eminönü ⓦ namlipastirma.com.tr.

One of the best delicatessens in the city, established in 1929, it sells a very wide range of cheeses from across the country (and some imported), a cornucopia of cured meats, including garlicky *pastırma* (a form of pastrami) and *sucuk* (a spicy sausage ring traditionally sliced and cooked up with eggs), as well as more prosaic items like olives, olive oil and pickles.

Tatlıcı Safa

MAP P.44, POCKET MAP F5
Hasırcılar Cad 10 ⊙ 1 Eminönü. ☎ 0212 527 2277.

Not so famous as *Karaköy Güllüoğlu* across the Golden Horn and consequently considerably cheaper, this is a great place to stock up on walnut-filled *baklava* or *fıstık sarması*, rolls of paper-thin filo pastry wrapped around a delicious pistachio filling. They also do more inexpensive favourites such as *tulumba*, a kind of corrugated donut roll soaked in syrup.

Kurukahveci Mehmet Efendi

Cafés

Konyalı

MAP P.44, POCKET MAP G6
Ankara Cad 4 ⓘ 1 Sirkeci ⓣ 0212 527 1935.

Opposite the entrance to Sirkeci Station, this traditional *pastane* has been supplying breakfasts, lunches and on-the-way-home snacks to local office workers and traders for decades. The tea comes in tulip-shaped glasses and there's a wide range of bread-based delights to choose from, such as bagel-like sesame seed-studded *simit* and lasagne-like *su böreği*, layers of boiled pastry filled with goat's cheese and parsley. Attached is the sister *Konyalı Lokantası*, a traditional Turkish restaurant dating back to 1897. €€

Lezzet-i Şark

MAP P.44, POCKET MAP F5
Hasırcılar Cad 38 ⓘ 1 Eminönü ⓣ 0212 514 2763.

Unsophisticated but excellent bazaar eating establishment dishing up delicious specialities from Gaziantep, Turkey's food capital.

Start off with bulgur wheat-wrapped meatballs (*içli köfte*) and finish with the sweetened cheese and shredded wheat dessert *künefe* – perhaps with a succulent kebab sandwiched between. No alcohol. €

Set Üstü Çay Bahçesi

MAP P.44, POCKET MAP J6
Gülhane Parkı ⓘ 1 Gülhane ⓣ 0212 513 9610.

This open-air café is rarely visited by tourists as it is hidden away in the northeast corner of Gülhane Park, near the Goths' Column. This is a shame as the tea here, brought to the table samovar-style, is delicious and the views across to Asia and up the Bosphorus are lovely. It also does basic food including *köfte* (grilled meatballs) and toasted sandwiches. €

Tarihi Eminönü Balık Ekmek

MAP P.44, POCKET MAP E5
Turyol İskele Yanı ⓘ 1 Eminönü ⓣ 0216 541 0352.

Set up right on the quay front just to the left of the entrance to the Galata Bridge, this simple café has combined tradition – it began

Tarihi Eminönü Balık Ekmek

across the Bosphorus in Asia in 1948 – with twenty-first-century business savvy, relocating to its present location in 2007 to take advantage of the huge numbers of visitors milling around the Eminönü waterfront. Enjoy a cheap fish sandwich served by staff in faux-Ottoman brocade-decorated attire. €

Restaurants

Hamdi et Lokantası

MAP P.44, POCKET MAP F5
Kalçın Sok 17 ⓘ 1 Eminönü
Ⓦ hamdi.com.tr.

Set back from the Eminönü waterfront, this traditional restaurant specializing in southeast Turkish food serves up some of the best kebabs (over twenty varieties of them) and accompaniments in the central part of the old city, and has quality *baklava* for dessert. Tables on the upper floors of this five-storey establishment have good views across the Galata Bridge and Golden Horn. It's expensive by kebab-joint standards and some diners have reported off-hand service. Licensed. €€

Kybele

MAP P.44, POCKET MAP G11
Yerebatan Cad 23 ⓘ 1 Sultanahmet
ⓘ 0212 511 7766.

The uniquely eccentric ambiance of this restaurant is something unforgettable and magical. There are countless lamps in the ceiling, stacks of trinkets and intricate carpets on the floors, and it feels as if you've entered an old Turkish fairytale. Upstairs there's a beautiful terrace too. Take a seat in one of the nooks and crannies of the spacious interior and enjoy a traditional meal. €€

Orient Express Restaurant

MAP P.44, POCKET MAP H6
İstasyon Cad, Sirkeci Gar 2
Ⓦ orientexpressrestaurant.net.

This nineteenth-century, European-designed restaurant is based inside Sirkeci Station, which was in the not too distant past the last stop for the world-famous Orient Express. It's a truly atmospheric location to tuck into a variety of traditional Turkish dishes. Kebabs, *köfte* and stuffed vegetables are standard. The restaurant is licensed too, with wine by the glass and beers available, though prices are steep compared to the food. €

Pandeli's

MAP P.44 POCKET MAP F6
No: ½ Mısır Çarşısı 1 ⓘ 1 Eminönü ⓘ 0212 527 3909.

An Istanbul institution founded in 1890 and atmospherically located on the second floor of the bustling Spice Bazaar. Set up by an Anatolian Greek shepherd who forsook his flocks for the big city, the signature dish is *hünkar beğendi* (the sultan liked it), comprising a creamy, smoked aubergine base topped by succulent lamb stew. The attractive blue tile work dates back to its establishment, and everyone from Queen Elizabeth II to Audrey Hepburn has eaten here. €€

Bar

Kardelen Pub

MAP P.44 POCKET MAP H10
Muradiye Cad 3 ⓘ 1 Gülhane ⓘ 0212 522 8393.

Given the paucity of bars in this area, the *Kardelen* makes a welcome, if gritty, haven for a beer or two after a day's sightseeing. Perched up above the T1 tram track, it's always busy serving a mix of visitors and commuters streaming from the metro at Sirkeci Station. If you get drawn into the atmosphere, there's reasonable *meyhane* style meals to be had for good prices.

Grand Bazaar District

This sprawling area of the old city contains one of Istanbul's best-known and most-visited buildings, the ever-busy Grand Bazaar, reputedly the largest covered historic bazaar in the world – and fifteenth-century forerunner of today's shopping malls. Its real jewel, however, stands in imposing grandeur on top of the third hill of the old city – the Süleymaniye, a mosque complex of near architectural perfection. Viewing the silhouette of its cascading domes and bristling minarets from across the Golden Horn at sunset is stunning, and an intimate walk around its hallowed grounds is moving. North and west of the Grand Bazaar, a rather grittier area – merging into the business district of Aksaray, is embellished by some important Ottoman mosques along with a few Byzantine-era gems, which are all the more enjoyable to explore as so few visitors make the effort to get off the beaten track.

Süleymaniye Mosque Complex

Süleymaniye Mosque Complex (Süleymaniye Külliyesi)

MAP P.60, POCKET MAP E6
Prof Siddik Sami Onar Cad, Vefa
🚋 1 Beyazıt or Laleli/Üniversite Ⓜ 2 Vezneciler ☎ 0212 514 0139.

Northwest of the Grand Bazaar, the Süleymaniye Külliyesi (mosque complex) is best reached by walking up from the Laleli/Üniversite tramstop, first along Büyük Resit Paşa Caddesi, then onto 16 Mart Şehit and Süleymaniye Caddesi. En route you'll pass the **Kalenderhane Camii**, a distinctive brick-built mosque once the thirteenth-century Byzantine Church of Kyriotissa, and under an arch of the fourth-century Aqueduct of Valens (see page 66). At the top is **Tıryakı Çarşısı**, "market of the addicts", a street in front of the mosque named after the opium addicts who puffed away their lives here. You are now in the **Süleymaniye Mosque Complex,** a group of buildings with the mosque at its heart, arguably the pinnacle of achievement of the architect Sinan, and worthy legacy of the sultan who founded it, Süleyman the Magnificent. Begun in 1550 on a tricky hilltop site, it took seven years to complete. Entering the **Süleymaniye Camii** by the side door, it's hard not to be impressed by the sheer sense of space the architect has achieved by cleverly hiding the piers supporting the massive dome (53m high by 26.5m in diameter) in the colonnaded supporting walls, adding half domes to the west and east and piercing the arched tympanum walls on the other two sides with rows of windows. It may be virtually the same plan as the Haghia Sophia, which was clearly its inspiration, but Sinan makes it his own achievement, especially as the interior is so gloriously austere. İznik tiles are used with great restraint, the marble-clad prayer niche (*mihrab*) and pulpit (*mimber*) are simple in design and the painted arabesque panels on the plasterwork muted in colour.

Outside, in the southeastern grounds of the mosque are the *türbe*s or **tombs** of Süleyman the Magnificent and his wife Haseki Hürrem or Roxelana (free). Süleyman's is an octagonal marble drum with a domed roof; inside is the cenotaph of the greatest Ottoman sultan. Ranged in an L-shape around the southwest and northwest sides of the mosque are *medrese*s, a hospital

and a caravanserai for travellers – all once integral parts of this great philanthropic complex. The baths built as part of the complex are excellent and open to mixed bathing (**Süleymaniye Hamamı**, Mimar Sinan Cad 20 ⓦ suleymaniyehamami.com).

Grand Bazaar (Kapalı Çarşı)

MAP P.60, POCKET MAP F7
Beyazıt Ⓜ 1 Beyazıt or Çemberlitaş Ⓣ 0212 519 1248.

Known in Turkish as the Kapalı Çarşı or Covered Bazaar, this great shopping complex was originally built not long after the Ottoman Turkish conquest of the city in 1453, on the site of a Byzantine precursor. Like all bazaars in the Ottoman Empire, it was an open area in the beginning, centred on the *bedesten*, a lockable, covered (usually domed) building where valuable goods were stored. The commercial hub of the Grand Bazaar comprised two *bedesten*, the İç Bedesten, today containing jewellery and other shops, and the Sandal Bedesteni, not built until the sixteenth century, which was used for storing precious fabrics.

Up to half a million shoppers, both visitors and locals, visit the bazaar daily. If you're unused to Middle Eastern ways it can be a little intimidating, not only because of the importuning of a few of the owners of its four thousand or so shops, but also owing to the maze-like meanderings of the **66 vaulted**

The genius of Sinan

By far the most brilliant and prolific Ottoman architect, Sinan was a Christian by birth. Swept up in the annual *devişirme*, a levy of Christian youth taken into the sultan's service and compelled to convert to Islam, he was trained at the Topkapı Palace. In 1536, Sinan became imperial architect and is responsible for some 81 mosques, fifty theological schools, thirty-two palaces and numerous other structures, from bridges to hospitals – 321 in total. A devout Muslim and simple family man, he lived on site with his family while the Süleymaniye complex was under construction. He was buried here, aged 97, in a tomb, fittingly, he designed himself.

Grand Bazaar district

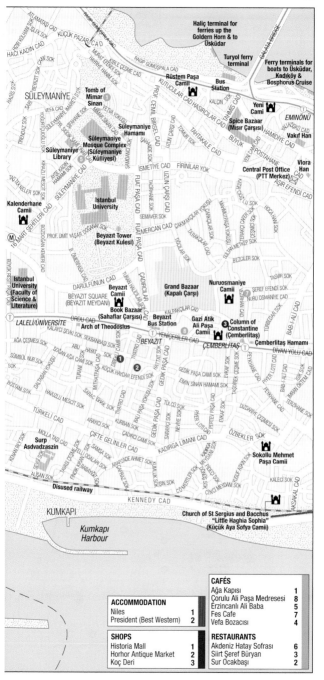

ACCOMMODATION

| Niles | 1 |
| President (Best Western) | 2 |

SHOPS

Historia Mall	1
Horhor Antique Market	2
Koç Deri	3

CAFÉS

Ağa Kapısı	1
Çorulu Ali Paşa Medresesi	8
Erzincanlı Ali Baba	5
Fes Cafe	7
Vefa Bozacısı	4

RESTAURANTS

Akdeniz Hatay Sofrası	6
Siirt Şeref Büryan	3
Sur Ocakbaşı	2

streets (the name-plaques of which are often hidden beneath displays) and the sheer crush of people at busy times. It's also easy to exit by the "wrong" one of the twenty gates puncturing its walls and end up, disorientated, in an unfamiliar labyrinth of alleyways – some of which are still lined by workshops producing goods for the bazaar. In addition to shops, there's a plethora of **cafés and restaurants**, a mosque, moneychangers and banks, and essential, given the incredibly high annual turnover in gold here, market police known as *zabita*. Fortunately, the variety of goods on display, from exquisite gold and silver jewellery, antique carpets and flat-weave rugs (kilims) to fake designer clothes and accessories and gaudy belly-dancer outfits, keeps most people entertained, the majority of shop owners pleasant and friendly, and some of the eating places more than reasonable.

Book Bazaar (Sahaflar Çarşısı)

MAP P.60, POCKET MAP E7
Sahaflar Çarşısı Sok ⊙ 1 Beyazıt.
Reachable either from the southwest corner of the Grand Bazaar or from Beyazıt Square, this famous booksellers' market dates back to the Byzantine period. No longer the best place to hunt for secondhand or antiquarian rarities, it concentrates on academic tomes for students from nearby Istanbul University, and has a fair smattering of decent books on Istanbul in English.

Nuruosmaniye Camii

MAP P.60, POCKET MAP F7
Vezirhan Cad ⊙ 1 Çemberlitaş.
More or less opposite the Çarşı Kapısı gate on the east side of the Grand Bazaar, this attractive building, built between 1748 and 1755, was the first of the city's mosques to be influenced by the

The Grand Bazaar

SHOPS
Abdulla	3
Abdullah Şalabi	7
Adnan & Hasan	4
Derviş	5
Dhoku	6
Şişko Osman	2
Sivaslı İstanbul Yazmacı	1
Tradition	8

CAFÉS
Bedesten	4
Dönerci Şahin Üsta	3
Fes Cafe	2

RESTAURANTS
Aynen Dürüm	5
Havuzlu	6
Pedaliza Lokantası	1
Subaşı Lokantası	7

N

0 metres 50
0 yards 50

Baroque style. The prayer hall is little more than an impressively high central dome supported by four great bricked-in arches filled by windows, which flood the interior with light and make its name, the "Sacred Light of Osman", particularly apt. Flanked by twin cylindrical minarets, the mosque has a rare grace, especially as it is fronted by an elegant semicircular, rather than the usual square, courtyard. Due to its proximity to the Grand Bazaar, it is invariably very busy, especially at Friday midday prayers, and its pleasant courtyard, shaded by spreading plane trees, offers a peaceful respite to busy shoppers and workers.

Column of Constantine (Çemberlitaş)

MAP P.60, POCKET MAP F8
Yeniçeriler Cad ⊙ 1 Çemberlitaş.
Rising above all the domed Ottoman buildings hereabouts, this is a reminder of an earlier, Byzantine past, when this 35m-high column presided over the great oval Forum of Constantine. Erected by Constantine to commemorate the inauguration of his new city in 330, it was surmounted by a massive statue of the emperor himself, dressed as Apollo, which was toppled by a storm in 1106. Its Turkish name Çemberlitaş, or "hooped stone", refers to the reinforcing iron rings clamped around the joints of its ten porphyry drums following an earthquake in 416. It is sometimes called the "burnt column" after it was scorched by a great fire in 1179.

Çemberlitaş Hamamı

MAP P.60, POCKET MAP F8
Vezirhan Cad 8 ⊙ 1 Çemberlitaş
ⓦ cemberlitashamami.com.tr. Charge.
Opposite the Column of Constantine, this historic bathhouse is one of the three most popular in the old city and well used to foreign visitors. It was founded in the sixteenth century by Nur Banu Valide Sultan. An Italian by birth, she had been seized from the Greek island of Paros and brought to Istanbul to be a concubine in the *harem*. Eventually she ended up as consort to Selim II (1566–74) and mother to Sultan Murat III (1574–95). It follows the usual pattern of the city's Ottoman hamams and certainly makes an atmospheric and very conveniently located introduction to the Turkish bath ritual.

Gazi Atik Ali Paşa Camii

MAP P.60, POCKET MAP F8
Yeniçeriler Cad ⊙ 1 Çemberlitaş.
Often overlooked in favour of more imposing rivals such as the Blue and Süleymaniye mosques, the Gazi Atik Ali Paşa Camii, located a short way west along the tramline from the Column of Constantine, is important, as it is one of Istanbul's oldest mosques. Constructed in 1496 by a eunuch who became grand vizier and whose name the mosque bears, it consists of a 12m-diameter dome seated on the walls of the main body of the prayer hall, extended

Grand Bazaar

Beyazıt Square

by a semi-dome covering another section of the mosque containing the Mecca-facing *mihrab*.

Beyazıt Square (Beyazıt Meydanı)

MAP P.60, POCKET MAP E7
Ordu Cad ⊕ 1 Beyazıt.

Flanked to the west by the Grand Bazaar, to the south by traffic-filled Ordu Caddesi and to the north by the grounds of Istanbul University, this large square is one of the few (relatively speaking in this congested city) oases of peace in central Istanbul. The imperial mosque that gives the square its name, the **Beyazıt Camii**, was completed in 1506, making it the second oldest imperial mosque in the city. It's splendidly austere in style, with the usual colonnades ranged around three sides of the courtyard, supported by pillars of fine marble and centred on a pretty, octagonal ablutions fountain. The prayer hall of the mosque is exactly the same dimensions as the courtyard, making for a pleasing symmetry, and the central dome is abutted to the west and east by semi-domes, giving it the same spacious feel as

the Haghia Sophia and Süleymaniye Camii. Walking northwest across the pigeon-filled square, you soon come to the massive, ornamental gate of Istanbul University, one of the most prestigious in Turkey. Visible beyond it, in the grounds, is a striking white building, the **Beyazıt Tower** (Beyazıt Kulesi in Turkish), erected in 1828, which once served as a fire watchtower. The **Museum of Calligraphy**, housed in an Ottoman-era *medrese* in the northwest corner of the square, has been closed for many years. On the south side of the tramline and busy main road from the southwest corner of the square is a tangle of fallen columns, relief-carved with striking tear-drop motifs. This is all that remains of the once-monumental **Arch of Theodosius**, a triumphal arch that spanned the main road into the city centre, and marking the western entrance to what was once the largest forum or public space in Constantinople, the Forum of Theodosius I (379–395).

Laleli Camii

MAP P.60, POCKET MAP D7
Ordu Cad ⊕ 1 Aksaray.

It's worth continuing west from Beyazıt Square down traffic-clogged Ordu Caddesi to see the attractively ornate Laleli Camii, a mosque built in the Ottoman Baroque style between 1759 and 1763, during the reign of Mustafa II. As an imperial mosque, it used to be surrounded by a number of other buildings which served the surrounding community. The most obvious survivor of these is the attractive *sebil* or street fountain, which once dispensed water to the local populace. The mosque's graceful Baroque curves are best viewed from the exterior, but step inside to admire the plethora of columns supporting the main dome and galleries.

Şehzade Camii

MAP P.60, POCKET MAP D6
Şehzadebaşı Cad ⓣ 1 Laleli/Üniversite ⓜ 2 Vezneciler.

This, the Mosque of the Prince, is named in honour of Prince Mehmet, eldest son of Süleyman the Magnificent, who died in 1543 at the tender age of 21. It's another work of Sinan, and although most experts do not rate it as among his best, for the average visitor it is one of the most attractive – at least when viewed from the outside. Completed in 1548, the interior is very plain, with a central dome supported by four piers flanked by four semi-domes, giving it a trefoil plan. Outside, the courtyard is very satisfying aesthetically, with the porticoes surrounding all four sides roofed with a total of 16 small domes. But it's the twin minarets that really catch the eye, with their ribbing and low-relief-carved geometric patterns.

Istanbul Municipality Building (İstanbul Belediye Sarayı)

MAP P.60, POCKET MAP D7
Şehzadebaşı Cad ⓣ 1 Laleli/Üniversite.

Important as the first International Modern building in the old city, the design for this 1950s classic was by architect Nevzat Erol. Comprising a typical modernist-style eight-storey office block with a grid facade raised on columns, it is fronted by a meeting hall-cum-reception area surmounted by an unusual cross-arched roof. It may be at odds

Şehzade Camii

Aqueduct of Valens

with its ancient surroundings, but it is certainly striking.

Aqueduct of Valens

MAP P.60, POCKET MAP C6–D6
Atatürk Bulvarı ☉ 1 Aksaray Ⓜ 2 Vezneciler.

Spanning traffic-clogged Atatürk Bulvarı in two-tiered, 18.5m-high splendour, this aqueduct was in use from its construction around 375 under Emperor Valens through to the nineteenth century. Water was brought from various sources outside the city, piped under the land walls and all the way to the fourth hill, where a major valley between it and the third hill (where the Süleymaniye mosque complex now stands) meant a raised aqueduct was needed – the splendid construction you see today. From a storage reservoir near Beyazıt Square the water was distributed throughout the city. It's possible to follow its ever-decreasing height west from Atatürk Bulvarı to near the **Kalenderhane Camii** (see page 58), perhaps pausing for unusual refreshments at the wonderful *Vefa Bozacısı* (see page 69) en route.

Grand Bazaar shopping tips

Few goods bear price labels in the Grand Bazaar, so for most things you'll have to haggle. Before beginning negotiations for a particular item, ask the price of identical or similar items at other stores to give a ball-park figure. Then offer considerably less than the trader is asking (he'll likely be asking far more than he will accept). Walking away is a tactic that sometimes produces results but remember that once you've begun to bargain seriously it is rude not to pursue the process to the end – and not to buy once you've agreed a price is very bad form. The price of gold and silver jewellery fluctuates on a daily basis with prices for items based on the going rate – the jeweller should base his asking price on the weight of the piece you are interested in.

Shops: Grand Bazaar

Abdulla

MAP P.62, POCKET MAP F7
Halıcılar Cad 53 🚇 1 Beyazıt or Çemberlitaş
Ⓦ abdulla.com.

The fixed prices make this a popular bet with visitors, drawn in by the elegant displays of scarves, pastel-coloured cotton bath wraps, plump traditional towels, mohair rugs and all manner of handmade olive-oil soaps.

Abdullah Şalabi

MAP P.62, POCKET MAP F7
Cevahir Bedesteni 143–151 🚇 1 Beyazıt or Çemberlitaş 🕿 0212 520 2250.

Great little antiques stall established in 1880, stocking a wide range of curios and presided over by knowledgeable English-speaker Pol Şalabi. One speciality is icons.

Adnan & Hasan

MAP P.62, POCKET MAP F7
Halıcılar Cad 89–92 🚇 1 Beyazıt or Çemberlitaş Ⓦ adnanandhasan.com.

Long-established carpet and kilim purveyor stocking everything from very expensive Hereke carpets to moderately priced Anatolian and Caucasian kilims.

Derviş

MAP P.62, POCKET MAP F7
Keseciler Cad 51 🚇 1 Beyazıt or Çemberlitaş Ⓦ dervis.com.

Choose from a well-displayed array of silk scarves, cotton bath towels and robes, pashmina scarves, natural soaps and, more unusually, antique kaftans from Central Asia.

Dhoku

MAP P.62, POCKET MAP F7
Takkeciler Sok 52–60 🚇 1 Beyazıt or Çemberlitaş 🕿 0212 527 6841.

The concept is contemporary ethnic, hence the beautiful range of flat-weave kilims with strikingly modern geometric designs which often look far better at home than more traditional rugs.

Koç Deri

MAP P.60, POCKET MAP F7
Tavuk Pazarı Sk 27 🚇 1 Beyazıt or Çemberlitaş 🕿 0212 527 5533.

Leather goods are as traditionally Turkish in origin as carpets and İznik pottery, and this place sells some of the best-quality jackets, bags and other accessories in the city.

Şişko Osman

MAP P.62, POCKET MAP F7
Zincirli Han 🚇 1 Beyazıt or Çemberlitaş Ⓦ siskoosman.com.

A rambling store presided over by the knowledgeable and voluble Şişko (Fat) Osman, stocking all manner of antique carpets and kilims. Come here for apple tea and an entertaining soft-sell.

Sivaslı Istanbul Yazmacı

MAP P.62, POCKET MAP F7
Yağlıkcılar Cad 🚇 1 Beyazıt or Çemberlitaş 🕿 0212 526 7748.

This textile cornucopia, sometimes known as Necdet Danış, has been making quality *peştemals* (Turkish

Adnan & Hasan

bath towels), tablecloths and scarves, as well as stunning fabrics, for over 40 years. Well regarded by locals for quality goods at fair prices.

Tradition

MAP P.62, POCKET MAP F7
Rubiye Han 11/12, Kürkçüler Sok
☎ 0212 520 7907.

Opened in 1988 and co-run by Frenchwoman Florence Heilbron, this excellent establishment has a very good reputation, plenty of repeat customers (including a coterie of French diplomats and politicians) and sells pieces from €50 to €10,000.

Shops: Aksaray

Historia Mall

MAP P.60, POCKET MAP B6
Adnan Menderes Bulvarı. Buses #38, #39, #55EB ⓦ www.historia.com.tr.
Handily located next to the excellent *Akdeniz Hatay Sofrası* restaurant (see page 70), this shopping mall is tricky to reach (your best bet from Sultanahmet is to take the T1 tram to the Aksaray stop, and then take a fifteen-minute walk). Spread over four floors are international favourites such as Levi and Converse, along with good Turkish fashion outlets like Mavi (selling jeans etc) and Derimod (which specialises in leather). One floor is taken up by a food court.

Horhor Antique Market

MAP P.60, POCKET MAP C7
Yorum Kırık Tulumba Sok 13/22
ⓜ 1 Aksaray ☎ 0212 525 9977.
Out-of-the-way location, but easy enough to reach from the Aksaray T1 tramstop, this massive antiques centre has all manner of wares displayed on five floors, much of it imported from Europe in the nineteenth and early twentieth centuries. You'll have to hunt and haggle hard for a real bargain though.

Cafés

Ağa Kapısı

MAP P.60, POCKET MAP E6
Nazir Hizmet Efendi Sok 11 ⓜ 1 Laleli/ Üniversite ⓜ 2 Vezneciler ⓦ facebook.com/ AgaKapisi.
If you're visiting the Süleymaniye complex, don't miss this great café hidden on an alley below Sinan's tomb. The views of the Golden Horn and Galata Bridge are as unexpected as they are superb. Try an Ottoman fruit sherbert, Turkish coffee or *gözleme*, a paratha-like bread-round stuffed with cheese or potato, or even a puff on a *nargile* on the upper floor – all usually in the company of students from the university. €

Bedesten

MAP P.62, POCKET MAP F7
Cevahir Bedesteni 143–151 ⓜ 1 Çemberlitaş ☎ 0212 520 2250.
Tucked away in the Cevahir Bedesteni in the heart of the Grand Bazaar, this well-run and stylish place makes a great spot to rest up between shopping bouts. Well-priced food is a mix of Turkish (try the yoghurt-drenched Turkish ravioli, *mantı*) and international (brownies and cheesecake), and the coffee is good. The decor is special too, dominated by two giant *alem*, the brass crescent and star finials that adorn mosque domes and minarets. €

Çorulu Ali Paşa Medresesi

MAP P.60, POCKET MAP F7
Ali Baba Türbe Sok Medrese, Yeniçeriler Cad 36–38 ⓜ 1 Beyazıt ☎ 0212 528 3785.
Housed in the Çorulu Ali Paşa Medrese, the *Erenler Çay Bahçesi* is a great place to stop for a bargain-priced traditional Turkish *çay* (tea) sipped from a tiny, tulip-shaped glass, or to toke on a *nargile* (water pipe). €

Dönerci Şahin Üsta

MAP P.62, POCKET MAP F7

Nuruosmaniye Kılıçlar Sok 7 ⊙ 1
Çemberlitaş ⊙ 0212 526 5297.

Most visitors pass this hole in the
wall, stand-up *döner* kebab joint
thinking it's just another cheap
place dishing up bland, pre-
prepared *döner*s brought in from
outside. It isn't, as the queues of
loyal regulars attest. Enjoy tender
lamb painstakingly layered on
the vertical spit each morning,
grilled to perfection, then sliced
onto a small *pide* bread and served
with juicy tomatoes and sumac-
smothered onion. €

Erzincanlı Ali Baba

MAP P.60, POCKET MAP E6
Sidik Sami Onar Cad 11 ⊙ 1 Laleli/
Üniversite ⊙ 0212 514 5878.

Overlooking the Süleymaniye
mosque and with tables out on the
"market of the addicts", this is an
ideal lunch stop – especially if you
like the beans (*kuru fasulye*) which
have made it famous. Tender,
buttery, dripping with tomato
sauce and topped by a spicy
pepper, a bowl of these cheap and
delicious pulses is a delight. They
also do a range of other Turkish
dishes. €

Fes Cafe

MAP P.62, POCKET MAP F7
Ali Baba Türbe Sok 25/7A, off
Nuruosmaniye Cad ⊙ 1 Çemberlitaş
Ⓦ facebook.com/fescafe.

Just outside the Grand Bazaar
and with a smaller branch
inside on Halıcılar Cad 62, this
contemporary take on a traditional
Turkish café serves up good
sandwiches and cakes to a mainly
middle-class Turkish clientele. Also
does very decent coffee. €

Vefa Bozacısı

MAP P.60, POCKET MAP D6
Katip Çeşebi Cad 104/1 ⊙ 1 Laleli/
Üniversite Ⓜ 2 Vezneciler Ⓦ vefa.com.tr.

Whether you like the traditional
speciality *boza*, a viscous
fermented millet drink topped by
connoisseurs with roasted chickpeas
(bought from a shop across the
road), is almost beside the point,
as the ambience of the delightful
interior is what counts. Caught in
an early twentieth-century time-
warp, it's all dark-wood shelves and
cut-glass mirrors. Slightly sweet and
fizzy, *boza* is delicious – Atatürk
himself thought so and the glass he
drank from in the 1930s is proudly

Çorlulu Ali Paşa Medresesi

GRAND BAZAAR DISTRICT

on display on one wall. You can also stock up on chunky souvenir bottles of *nar suyu* (pomegranate syrup) and *üzüm sirkesi* (grape vinegar). €

Restaurants

Akdeniz Hatay Sofrası

MAP P.60, POCKET MAP B6
Ahmediye Cad 44/A. Buses #38, #55/EB
☏ 0212 531 3333.

Unpromisingly located place specializing in the Arabinfluenced food of the Syrian-border province of Hatay, this is nonetheless one of the city's best restaurants. There's an extensive range of meze ranging from *zahter*, a thyme-based salad, to hummus topped by *pastırma* (pastrami) or pine nuts, and spectacular mains like *tuzda tavuk*, a whole chicken stuffed with fragrant pilaf rice, oven-roasted in a thick salt coating and brought to the table flaming. Just as ostentatiously delicious are the metre-long kebabs. Unlicensed. €

Aynen Dürüm

MAP P.62, POCKET MAP F7

Muhafazacilar Sok 33 ⓘ 1 Çemberlitaş
☏ 0212 527 4728.

If you prefer a quick bite to go, grab a sandwich at this little gem. Both locals and tourists queue here and sit at a street pew with a kebab wrap in hand. The liver sandwich is top, but any type of meat you choose is delicious. The quality speaks for itself – this is street food at its best. Definitely worth the wait. €

Havuzlu

MAP P.62, POCKET MAP F7
Gani Çelebi Sok 3 ⓘ 1 Çemberlitaş
ⓦ havuzlurestaurant.com.

Brisk-bordering, brusque-service is the order of the day in this Grand Bazaar institution, appreciated by locals for its good-quality kebabs and hearty stews and by visitors for the atmospheric dining room beneath a four-hundred-year-old vaulted ceiling. Choose from over twenty varieties of *sulu yemek* (stew-type dishes) laid out in a giant steamtray and changing daily, with desserts including *sutlaç* (oven-baked rice pudding) and *kabak tatlısı* (candied pumpkin). Unlicensed. €

Fes Cafe

Havuzlu

Pedalıza Lokantası

MAP P.62, POCKET MAP F7
Yğlıkcılar Cad, Cebeci Han ⓘ 1 Çemberlitaş
ⓘ 0212 522 4333.

Gem of a place located in a
vaulted brick trade hall (*han*),
with white-shirted waiters, a
bustling atmosphere (especially
at lunchtime) and great dishes
including *kağıt kebab* (lamb oven-
baked between grease proof paper),
and a good selection of fragrant-
rice stuffed vegetables. €

Siirt Şeref Büryan

MAP P.60, POCKET MAP E6
İtfaiye Cad 4. Bus #38 ⓘ 0212 635 8085.

Nestling in the shadow of the
Aqueduct of Valens, this is the
place to try the eastern Turkish
speciality *büryan*, lamb cooked
slowly in a clay *tandır* oven
or, even better, *perde pilaf*, a
delicious rice dish flavoured
with almonds, shredded chicken,
raisins and spices. Most of the
food shops on the fascinating
street on which it stands are run
by Kurds from the southeast of
Turkey and stock all manner of
cheeses, spices and other goodies.
Unlicensed. €

Subaşı Lokantası

MAP P.62, POCKET MAP F7
Nuruosmaniye Cad 48, Çarşı Kapı ⓘ 1
Çemberlitaş ⓘ 0212 522 4762.

Packed with traders from the
Grand Bazaar at lunchtimes,
this spit-and-sawdust *lokanta*
(traditional Turkish restaurant)
dishes up cheap and cheerful
stews from huge steamtrays as
well as *köfte* and kebabs. It's
conveniently located right outside
the main, Çarşı, gate to the
bazaar. Unlicensed. €

Sur Ocakbaşı

MAP P.60, POCKET MAP C6
İtfaiye Cad 27, Fatih Bus #38
ⓦ surocakbasi.com.

Fronting a lively pedestrianized
square, this down-to-earth
ocakbaşı is noted for its *saç tava*,
a rich fried meat and vegetable
stew usually eaten with copious
chunks of *pide* flatbread, as well
a startling array of kebabs, spicy
lahmacun and even the stuffed
intestine speciality *bumbar*.
The late TV chef and food
personality Anthony Bourdain
was brought here when he
visited the city. €

Northwest quarter and the land walls

Compelling yet seldom visited, the northwest quarter stands astride the fourth, fifth and sixth hills of the old city. Best explored on foot, its narrow streets, the most evocative running steeply down to the shores of the Golden Horn beneath strings of washing hung between once grand nineteenth-century apartments, are the beat of skullcapped conservative Muslim men and veiled women. Yet working churches survive, including the spiritual centre of the Orthodox Christian world, the Fener Greek Patriarchate, as well as Byzantine treasures like St Saviour in Chora, today the Kariye Museum, with its stunning mosaics and frescoes. The quarter is bounded to the northwest by the remarkably intact fifth-century land walls of Theodosius which, if followed south, run through yet more atmospheric districts dotted with interesting sights, finally ending by the coruscating waters of the Sea of Marmara.

Kariye Mosque

MAP P.74, POCKET MAP A2
Kariye Camii Sok Ⓜ1 Ulubatlı/Topkapı, buses #28, #36/V, #37/Y, #38, #38/E, #55/EB, #87 Ⓣ0212 631 9241. Charge, extra for audio-guide. Closed at the time of writing.
Out by the land walls of Theodosius, some 5km from the centre of the old city, the Byzantine **Church of St Saviour in Chora** was converted into a mosque, the Kariye Camii, after the Ottoman conquest. Later, as the **Kariye Museum**, it was the one absolute must-see historic site beyond Sultanahmet and its environs. Dating back to perhaps as early as the fourth century, it originally lay beyond the walls of Constantinople – hence "Chora", Greek for "in the country" – but the pretty brick-built building you see today dates largely from an eleventh-century rebuild followed, in the early fourteenth century, by a remodelling by prominent Byzantine statesman and scholar, **Theodore Metochites**. Crucially, the wealthy Metochites added the twin nartnexes (entrance vestibules) and the funerary chapel (parecclesion) to the church, home to the bulk of the mosaics and frescoes which make it so stunning. At the time of writing it was still closed after several years of restoration, with plans to re-open it as a working mosque, or possibly as a museum, so check the latest online before you visit.

Rezan Has Museum and Gallery (Rezan Has Müzesi)

MAP P.74, POCKET MAP D4
Kadir Has Üniversitesi. Bus #99, #99A & #99Y Ⓜ2 Haliç Ⓦrhm.org.tr. Charge.
This museum-cum-exhibition space is housed in Kadir Has University, once a nineteenth-century tobacco factory. A must for archeology buffs, a

series of cases exhibit exquisite finds from the Neolithic period through to the Selçuk Turkish era, atmospherically set out in a Byzantine cistern in the bowels of the university. The artefacts are mainly Anatolian and superb examples of their type – from Urartian metalwork to Hellenistic-era surgical equipment, seal stones to Roman figurines. The adjoining gallery hosts a mixed bag of exhibitions.

Church of the Pantocrator (Zeyrek Camii)

MAP P.74, POCKET MAP D5
İbadethane Sok, İtfaiye Cad. Buses #28, #28/T.

Converted into a mosque after the Ottoman conquest and still a mosque to this day, this fine late-Byzantine building stands on a hilltop above Atatürk Bulvarı. Built in 1136, it comprised two churches linked by a chapel. The interior retains some fine marble panels and opus sectile flooring of differently coloured marble pieces. A short walk southwest is the Kadınlar Pazarı (Women's Bazaar), home to a plethora of food shops run mainly by Kurds.

Fener Greek High School for Boys

MAP P.74, POCKET MAP B3
Sancaktar Yokuşu Sok 36, Fener Bus #99.

This imposing Victorian-Gothic building, built with bricks imported from France in 1883, is an unmissable sight on the slopes of the old city's fifth hill. There has been a school here since Byzantine times, but today it's hard not to view it without thinking about the precipitous decline of the Greek minority in the city since its construction. Then there were over 400,000 Greeks in a city with a population of around one million. Today, there are just 2,000 or so in a metropolis of seventeen million, and fewer than sixty pupils attend this cavernous school.

Frescoes in Kariye Mosque

The northwest quarter

Eyüp

metres 500
yards 500

Defterdar Ferry Terminal
FESHANE
Ayvansaray Ferry Terminal
NISANCA
N
Anemas Zındanları
Panghia Blachernae
Ivaz Efendi Camii
Eğrikapı
Palace of the Porphyrogenitus (Tekfur Sarayı)
Erdinekapı Cemetery
Edirne Kapı
Kariye Museum (Kariye Müzesi)
Ahrida Synagogue
Church of the Pammakaristos (Fethiye Camii/ Müzesi)
Mihrimah Camii
Church of the St Mary of the Mongols (Kanlı Kilisesi)
St Stephen of the Bulgars
Hasköy Ferry Terminal
AYVANSARAY
Haliç Park
BALAT
GOLDEN HORN
HASKÖY
Zindan Arkası Cemetery
Fener Orthodox Patriarchate (Fener Rum Patrikhanesi)
Rezan Has Museum and Gallery (Rezan Has Müzesi)
Fener Greek High School for Boys
FENER
Gül Camii
Yavuz Selim Camii
Cistern of Aspar
Sultan Sarnıcı
Eski İmaret Camii
Kadir Has University
FATİH
Church of the Pantocrator (Zeyrek Camii)
Fatih Camii
ZEYREK
Capa Hospital
Aqueduct of Valens
CAPA
EMNİYET FATİH
Şehzade Camii
İstanbul Municipal Building (İstanbul Belediye Sarayı)
AKSARAY
FINDIKZADE
AHMET VEFİKPAŞA CAD
Çukur Bostan
HASEKİ
Haseki Hospital
Valide Camii
Laleli Camii
AKSARAY
YUSUFPAŞA
Haseki Camii
Hekimoğlu Ali Paşa Camii
Ramazan Efendi Camii
Cerrahpaşa Hospital
Mesipaşa Camii
YENİKAPI
Havabus Airport Bus Stop
Disused railway
Yenikapı Waterfront Park
Yenikapı ferry terminal
SEA OF MARMARA

CAFÉS
Arnavüt Köfteci 1
Durak Rümeli Köfte Salonu 3

RESTAURANTS
Asitane 2
Develi 4

ACCOMMODATION
Troya Hotel Balat 1

Fatih Camii

MAP P.74, POCKET MAP C5
İslambol Cad. Buses #28,#28/T, #36/V, #37/Y, #38/E.

Northwest along the line of the aqueduct is the monumental and newly restored Fatih Camii (Mosque of the Conqueror). This impressive structure was Istanbul's first purpose-built (as opposed to a converted church) mosque. Finished in 1470, it was largely rebuilt after an earthquake in 1776. At the centre of the usual complex, this is the heart of the old city's most conservative district and bearded men in skullcaps are a common sight, as are chador-clad women. On Wednesdays the streets round about are home to Istanbul's most vibrant street market, the **Çarşamba Pazarı**.

Yavuz Selim Camii

MAP P.74, POCKET MAP C3
Yavuz Selim Cad. Buses #28, #28/T, #36/V, #37/Y, #38/E.

This austerely beautiful mosque lies northwest of the Fatih Camii, on the fifth hill. Its shallow single dome spans the prayer hall with sublime simplicity and İznik tiles are used with great restraint. Almost as impressive as the mosque are the splendid views from the attractive grounds, down over the Golden Horn and beyond. Behind the mosque the **tomb of Selim the Grim** (charge) is worth a look, as he was arguably the most successful Ottoman sultan, adding parts of Persia plus Syria, Palestine, Arabia and Egypt to the empire. He was known as "the Grim" for his habit of chopping off the heads of unsatisfactory grand viziers on a regular basis. The tomb retains a couple of superb tile panels.

The large, square hollow as you approach Yavuz Selim Camii used to function as the early Byzantine **Cistern of Aspar**, an open cistern once the largest of its kind in the city. Its brick-built retaining walls

Interior of Fatih Camii

are still partially visible. Also nearby, down narrow Ali Naki Sokak, is the **Sultan Sarnıcı**. This beautiful, covered **Byzantine cistern** is some 29m by 19m and has a brick-vaulted ceiling supported by marble pillars, each topped by a richly sculpted Corinthian capital. The cistern, now completely dry, functions as an atmospheric venue for wedding receptions and the like. Entry is free.

Church of the Pammakaristos (Fethiye Camii/Müzesi)

MAP P.74, POCKET MAP B3
Fethiye Cad. Bus #28. Charge. Closed for renovation until further notice.

Overshadowed by the nearby Kariye Mosque (see page 72), the **mosaics** in the funerary chapel of **the former Church of the Pammakaristos** are one of the "hidden" treasures of the city. The church was converted into a mosque in the late sixteenth century and still functions as one today, but the former chapel containing the mosaics has been turned into the **Fethiye Museum**. The typically brick-built domed building of the Byzantine church dates back to the twelfth century, while the chapel containing the mosaics was added in 1310. Well signed, the superbly preserved and vibrant mosaics include Christ Pantocrator in the dome, surrounded by the twelve Prophets, and a baptism scene showing Christ and John the Baptist. Between 1456 and 1587, this church was the Greek Orthodox Patriarchate.

Church of St Mary of the Mongols (Kanlı Kilisesi)

MAP P.74, POCKET MAP C3
Tevkii Cafer Mektebi Sok. Bus #99.

Reached either from the fifth hill above or the shores of the Golden Horn in Fener below, the unusual thirteenth-century Church of St Mary of the Mongols, in the shadow of the massive Fener Greek High School for Boys, is well worth a look. It's the only church in the city where Orthodox services have been carried out from the Byzantine period to the present day, but entry is dependent on the caretaker being at home.

Fener Orthodox Patriarchate (Fener Rum Patrikhanesi)

MAP P.74, POCKET MAP C3
Mursel Paşa Cad. T1 tram from Eminönü, Bus #99 ⓘ 0212 525 2117. Free.

On level ground close to the Golden Horn waterfront and stretches of the Byzantine sea walls that once ringed the peninsula and joined up with the land walls (see page 79), the Greek Orthodox Patriarchate remains, at least in theory, the spiritual centre of Orthodox Christians worldwide. The **Church of St George** at the heart of the complex, built in 1720, has a barrel-vaulted ceiling, an excess of gilt but one particularly

Fethiye Camii/Müzesi

St Stephen of the Bulgars

fine portable mosaic icon of the Virgin Mary.

St Stephen of the Bulgars

MAP P.74, POCKET MAP C2
Murel Paşa Cad 85–88. T1 tram from Eminönü, Bus #99. Free.

Stranded on a traffic island close to the waterfront, this church was constructed from cast-iron panels in Vienna in the late nineteenth century and floated down the Danube into the Black Sea and thence on to Istanbul. With its golden domes, it's very attractive, especially when viewed from the Haliç ferry. Major restoration was completed in 2017, and it is now a surprisingly busy attraction, popular with Instagrammers and other visitors.

Ahrida Synagogue

MAP P.74, POCKET MAP B2
Kürkçüçeşme Sok. T1 tram from Eminönü, Bus #99 ☎ 0212 243 5166. Contact the Chief Rabbinate at least one day before to arrange a visit. Free.

Hidden away in the backstreets of the atmospheric district of Balat, once home to a sizeable Jewish community, this originally fifteenth-century synagogue was rebuilt in Baroque style in 1694. The Jews have long since moved to other parts of the city or emigrated to Israel, but it receives a fair number of visitors despite the problems of having to arrange a visit in advance.

Yedikule Museum

MAP P.78
Kale Meydanı Cad. ☺ 1 train, buses #80, #80/T ☎ 0212 585 8933. Charge.

Wall-walking enthusiasts should start where the wall began, at the **Marble Tower** on the south side of traffic-filled Kennedy Caddesi. A short walk north on the outside of the walls is **Yedikule Gate** (Yedikule Kapı). Enter here as access to Yedikule Museum is on the inside of the walls. Essentially a fortress added to the line of the Byzantine walls by Mehmet the Conqueror in 1457–58, it consists of three large towers linked by a curtain wall and connected to a section of the land walls which boasts four towers of its own. This gives rise to the fortification's Turkish name Yedikule, "The

The Land Walls

Land walls of Theodosius

This superb feat of Byzantine engineering stretches some 6.5km, from the Sea of Marmara to the Golden Horn, thus cutting off the peninsula on which the city was built from the rest of Europe – and it kept foes as formidable as **Attila the Hun** and the Arab armies of Islam at wall's-width for a thousand years. Constructed as a single wall in 413 under Theodosius II, following a disastrous earthquake in 447 the defences were rebuilt in triplicate. The inner wall of the defences was now 5m thick and 12m high, strengthened by 96 towers; the outer wall 2m by 8.5m, again fortified by towers spaced between those on the main wall behind; in front lays a 20m-wide moat. **Walking** the line of the walls today is an adventure, with opportunities to mount the battlements and visit a number of other sights en route. Avoid leaving late in the day as the wall runs through some poor neighbourhoods, and petty theft is not unknown around dusk and after dark.

To get to the south end of the walls at Yedikule, take the #80 bus from Eminönü or the #80/T from Taksim. A much easier way is to take the Marmaray metro from Sirkeci to the Kazlıçeşme stop, just outside the walls near Yedikule. From the north end of the walls, the Haliç ferry runs down the Golden Horn from Ayvansaray to Eminönü, or take the #99 bus to the same destination.

Seven Towers". Yedikule was, ironically, given its appearance, never used as a fort. Two of its towers left of the entrance were in Ottoman times a prison and treasury, and the section of land walls incorporates the earlier, famous **Golden Gate**. This triple-arched structure, now bricked up, was a triumphal arch erected under Theodosius I in 390 over one of the main roads leading into Constantinople.

Belgrat Kapı

MAP P.78
Bus #93/T.

From **Yedikule Kapı**, it's possible to follow the outside of the partially restored walls northwards. The moat is now used for market gardens, but there are well-preserved sections of outer and inner wall. The next gate, **Belgrat (Belgrade) Kapı**, was originally a military gate that included portals through the inner and outer walls but did not have – as the public gates had – a bridge across the moat.

Zoodochus Pege Balikli Kilise

MAP P.78
Seyit Nizam Cad 3. Bus #93/T. Free.

Following the walls north you reach **Silivri Kapı**, known as Pege in Byzantine times because of the nearby shrine of **Zoodochus Pege**. Cross the busy six-lane highway paralleling the walls and follow a road 500m west through mixed Muslim and Christian cemeteries to a pretty nineteenth-century Greek church, built over a much earlier Byzantine structure. It's famed for the fish living in its *ayazma*, a sacred underground spring.

Panorama 1453 Museum (Panoramik Müze1453)

MAP P.78
Topkapı Kültür Parkı 1 Topkapı

Panaroma 1453 Museum

 panoramikmuze.com. **Charge, extra for audio-guide.**
North of Silivri Kapı is Mevlana Kapı. Northwest of this gate, across the six-lane highway in an area of urban park stranded in a major junction, is the Panorama 1453 Museum. Turks outnumber foreigners here, no doubt because the museum glorifies the iconic conquest of what was then Christian Constantinople by the Muslim, Ottoman Turks on 29 May 1453. Downstairs a circular viewing gallery runs beneath a large dome on which is cleverly painted – in an eye-boggling 360-degree panorama – the army of the young Sultan Mehmet I besieging the walls of Constantinople. Flaming balls of Greek fire, the Byzantines' "secret" weapon, pour down on the hapless attackers, who hold the green flag of Islam aloft in defiance, and the mighty walls crack and crumble under the assault of the Orban, a monster cannon over 8m long and with a bore wide enough to allow a man to crawl inside. The impressive scene, reputed to contain over 10,000 figures, is enhanced by a realistic battlefield tableau ringing the viewing gallery.

The Walls – Topkapı to Edirne Kapi

MAP P.78, POCKET MAP A1
Back across the busy thoroughfare from the Panorama 1453 Museum and on the north side of Millet Caddesi, which runs either side of the T1 tramline, is the Topkapı or **Gate of the Cannonball**, named after the Orban cannon that pulverized the land walls with shot weighing up to half a tonne. Continuing north you have to negotiate traffic-choked Adnan Menderes (Vatan) Caddesi – preferably by the underpass that also leads to the M1 Ulubatlı/Topkapı stop. Between here and Edirne Kapı is a pronounced dip, the valley of the

Lycus river, a weak point because the walls along the valley floor were lower than the besiegers' weaponry. This is where the Turks finally and decisively pierced the walls and poured into the city. The walls now run through Sulukule, a neighbourhood home to a **gypsy community** for centuries. Many of the traditional wood houses they inhabited have been controversially bulldozed by the municipality, with posh villas in walled compounds put in their place.

Mihrimah Camii

MAP P.74
Edirnekapı. Buses #28, #36/V, #37/Y, #38, #38/E, #55/EB.

Majestically located on the summit of the sixth of the old city's seven hills, this recently restored mosque is one of architect Sinan's (see page 59) earlier masterpieces. It was commissioned by Rüstem Paşa, grand vizier to Süleyman the Magnificent, and his wife Mihrimah, the sultan's favourite daughter. Access is via steps on the north side of the mosque. The beautiful prayer hall is incredibly light and airy due to the three rows of windows puncturing each of the four filled arches supporting the 20m-diameter dome. Just beyond the Mihrimah Camii is **Edirne Kapı** which bears, on the outside, a modern plaque in Turkish proclaiming it the entry point of the victorious Sultan Mehmet II on 29 May 1453.

Palace of the Porphyrogenitus (Tekfur Sarayı)

MAP P.74, POCKET MAP A2
Edirnekapı, Şişhane Cad. Buses #28, #36/V, #37/Y, #38, #38/E, #55/EB ☎ 0212 525 6130. Charge

The walls dip down towards the Golden Horn past Edirne Kapı. Built into the line, well-preserved here, is the **Tekfur Saray,** or

Palace of the Porphyrogenitus. Until 2014 a mere shell, this former annexe of the Blachernae Palace is now a museum concentrating primarily on one of the buildings later functions, as an Ottoman-era pottery known as Tekfur Sarayı. The palace marks the start of a change in the walls, now a single, thicker line bulging out to the west and running down the steep hill towards the Golden Horn, built in the seventh century.

Eyüp Camii

MAP P.74, POCKET MAP A1
Cami Kebir Sok. T1 tram from Eminönü, Buses #99, #39, or Haliç ferry.

A short walk north of the land walls is the district of Eyüp, named after Eyüp Ensari, standard bearer of the Prophet Mohammed, who died and was buried here during the first Arab siege of Constantinople (674–78). At the heart of the area the mosque bearing the standard bearer's name, and his tomb,

Mihrimah Camii

Tomb of Sokollu Mehmet Paşa

stand opposite each other across a courtyard – usually thronged with pilgrims. The mosque dates back to 1458 but was rebuilt in Baroque style in 1800 following an earthquake. The tomb (free) itself is covered in an eclectic mix of fine tiles. This is a sacred spot for Muslims – arguably the third most important Islamic pilgrimage site after Mecca and Jerusalem – and the whole area very conservative, so make sure you are modestly attired and women need to cover their heads in both mosque and tomb.

Tomb of Sokollu Mehmet Paşa

MAP P.74, POCKET MAP A1
Cami Kebir Cad. T1 tram from Eminönü, Buses #99, #39, or Haliç ferry.
A short way south of Eyüp Camii is a fine tomb, one of the many dotted around here. It houses the remains of Sokollu Mehmet Paşa, a Bosnian who became one of the empire's greatest grand viziers under Süleyman the Magnificent. The work of the leading architect of

the day, Sinan, it was completed in 1574. It's a beautiful work of art, a severe octagonal structure topped by a dome and embellished with some lovely stained glass. The other buildings ranged around it are part of the tomb complex and include a library, *medrese*, Koran school and the tombs of the grand vizier's family.

Eyüp Cemetery

MAP P.74, POCKET MAP A2
Gümüssuyu Karyağdı Sok. T1 tram from Eminönü, Buses #99, #39, or Haliç ferry.
On the prominent hill north of the mosque and tombs is a Muslim cemetery, thick with cypress trees standing sentinel over Ottoman-era, and much more recent and decidedly less ornate, tombstones. At the top is a very popular tea garden, the *Pierre Loti Café*, named after the French Romantic novelist who frequented the area in the late nineteenth century. A cable car (charge) links the banks of the Golden Horn, some 400m north of the Eyüp ferry quay, to the hilltop café.

Cafés

Arnavüt Köfteci

MAP P.74, POCKET MAP B2
Mursel Paşa Cad 139. Bus #99. ☏ 0212
531 6652.

A cult institution on the banks of
the Golden Horn, specializing in
cheap, tender grilled Albanian-style
meatballs (*köfte*). The attractive
European-style building dates back
to the nineteenth century when
this was a really cosmopolitan
neighbourhood, the eclectic slew of
formica-topped tables only came in
the 1950s – just a few years after the
place first opened its doors in 1947. €

Durak Rümeli Köfte Salonu

MAP P.74, POCKET MAP A3
Mihrimah Sultan Camii Altı 361. Bus #28,
#36/V, #37/Y, #38, #38/E, #55/EB ☏ 0212
587 9868.

Meatballs are a staple Turkish
fast food and this place does a
Macedonian-style *köfte* along with a
range of other good-value workers'
favourites like *kuru fasulye* (haricot
beans in tomato sauce). Set beneath
the lovely Mihrimah mosque with a
few outside tables. €

Restaurants

Asitane

MAP P.74, POCKET MAP A2
Kariye Hotel, Kariye Camii Sok 18
☏ 1 Topkapı/Ulubatlı or buses #28,
#36/V, #37/Y, #38, #38/E, #55/EB
⊕ asitanerestaurant.com.

Worth splashing out on, this
restaurant in the chestnut-tree-
shaded courtyard of the *Kariye Hotel*
(see page 137) was one of the
first places to revive Ottoman-style
cuisine, bringing new/old flavours
to foreigners and locals alike. Try
the *hünkar beğendi* (literally "the
sultan liked it"), an Ottoman classic
done to perfection here. Licensed.
Closed for renovation at the time of
writing. €€

Develi

MAP P.74, POCKET MAP A9
Gumuş Yüzük Sok 7 ⊕ 1 Kocamustafapaşa
☏ 0212 529 0833.

Founded in 1912 by émigrés
from the south of the country,
and it is still sizzling-out some of
the tenderest, tastiest meat in the
city. Overlooking an atmospheric
little square, the top-floor terrace
has great views over the Sea of
Marmara. The meze and *baklava*
are just as good as the wide range of
kebabs. Licensed. €€

Safa Meyhanesi

MAP P.78, POCKET MAP A9
İlyasbey Cad 12, Yedikule Marmaray
Ⓜ Kazlıçeşme, ☏ 0212 585 5594.

This delightful old school *meyhane*
looks like the stage set for a 1940s
movie, with its wooden walls, high
ceiling and glittering chandelier,
shelves of *rakı* bottles and the
original posters advertising this
potent aniseed spirit. It's a little out
of the way and has no live music so
it appeals to Istanbul intellectuals
and academics out for an evening.
Meze are good value; fish of the day
is priced by the kilo. €€

Asitane

Galata and the waterfront districts

Dominated by the landmark Galata Tower, which takes its name from the vibrant district at its feet, Galata's cobbled alleys tumble down to the busy north shore of the Golden Horn. An autonomous Genoese colony in the late Byzantine era, home to thriving Jewish, Moorish, Armenian and Greek communities since the Ottoman conquest, it has always been different from the conservative, mainly Muslim old city. Over the last decades it has blossomed from a run-down port area to a bohemian quarter of trendy shops, artists' studios, musicians' workshops, street art, hip bars and clubs. A quaint nineteenth-century underground funicular continues to toil up the hill and dervishes still whirl at the Galata Mevlevi Lodge.

Galata Tower (Galata Kulesi)

MAP P.86, POCKET MAP A15
Galata Meydanı ☎ 0212 249 0344. Charge.
Best reached by walking down Galip Dede Caddesi from İstiklal Tünel station, this soaring, 61m-high medieval tower, capped by a distinctive conical roof, was known as the Tower of Christ when it was built by the Genoese in 1349. Originally part of the fortification wall constructed to protect the Genoese mercantile colony established within it, it was turned into a jail in the fifteenth century. In the seventeenth century it was used, successfully, according to famous Ottoman traveller Evliya Çelebi, by pioneers experimenting in manned flight. From the eighteenth century, its purpose was more prosaic and pragmatic, as a watchtower for the then all too common fires. It is by far the biggest attraction in Galata, with long queues sometimes snaking around the square – particularly for the ever-popular sunset viewing period. The lookout gallery, reached today by a lift followed by two flights of stairs, is often crowded, but the views are worth it, with a foreground of the ferry-filled Golden Horn and manic Eminönü waterfront backed by the serene, mosque-lined skyline of the old city, all stately domes and elegant minarets.

Galata Mevlevi Lodge (Galata Mevlevihanesi)

MAP P.86, POCKET MAP A14
Galipdede Cad ⓦ muze.gen.tr. Charge.
This former lodge or monastery (*tekke*) of the Mevlevî Sufi order was home to one of Islam's mystical sects, the Mevlevîs. The order was founded in the thirteenth century by Mevlâna who, tired of the constraints of mainstream Sunni Islam, took his followers down the path of love and acceptance. Mevlâna's disciples, or dervishes, are best known in the West for their hypnotic rotating dance, hence "whirling dervish". This

ritual dance, along with prayer, meditation, contemplation and music, enabled adherents to achieve mystical union with God. The Mevlevîs, along with all Sufi orders, were deemed reactionaries by Atatürk and, in 1923, banned. The order went "underground" for decades but today is semi-officially tolerated. The lodge, built in the fifteenth century but much remodelled, is now a fascinating museum. Exhibits in the downstairs rooms, reached via a peaceful courtyard/ garden area, are arranged clockwise. Here, you can see the traditional instruments that provided the musical accompaniment to the dances, dervish costumes, begging bowls, kitchen utensils and a host of other interesting items. Upstairs is the *semahane*, where the dervishes whirled, a beautifully decorated, high-ceilinged octagonal room where dervish shows (charge) for visitors are held most Sundays at 6pm, with tickets sold online only in advance. Closed for restoration at the time of writing.

Ottoman Bank Museum/ SALT Gallery

MAP P.86, POCKET MAP A15

Bankalar Cad 35 ⓦ obmuze.com. Free.
Aptly situated on the "Street of Banks" and today owned by one of Turkey's leading banks, Garanti, this grandiose building was once the headquarters of the Ottoman Imperial Bank. The French architect behind this typically nineteenth-century European-style building was Vallaury, who also designed the Archeology Museum (see page 42) and *Pera Palace Hotel* (see page 138). Its cavernous interior has been cleverly modernized for Garanti Bank's **SALT contemporary arts project** and hosts a variety of temporary exhibitions. If the current exhibitions are not to your taste, it's worth perusing the permanent **Ottoman Bank Museum** on the ground floor. The bank served Galata's mainly non-Muslim, Greek, Armenian and Jewish inhabitants.

Around Bankalar Caddesi

MAP P.86, POCKET MAP A15

Dervishes, Galata Mevlevi Lodge

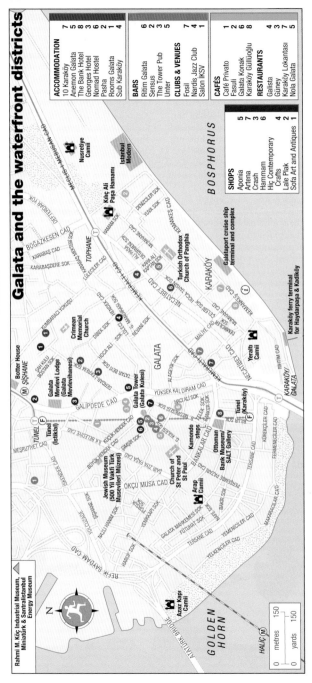

Galata and the waterfront districts

ACCOMMODATION	
10 Karaköy	7
Anemon Galata	5
The Bank Hotel	8
Georges Hotel	3
Nomad Hostel	6
Pasha	2
Rooms Galata	1
Sub Karaköy	4

BARS	
Ritim Galata	6
Sensus	2
The Tower Pub	3
Unter	5

CLUBS & VENUES	
Fosil	7
Nardis Jazz Club	4
Salon IKSV	1

CAFÉS	
Café Privato	1
Fasuli	2
Galata Konak	6
Karaköy Güllüoğlu	8

RESTAURANTS	
Galista	4
Güney	3
Karaköy Lokantası	7
Nola Galata	5

SHOPS	
Aponia	5
Artena	7
Crash	3
Hammam	6
Hiç Contemporary Crafts	4
Lale Plak	2
Sofa Art and Antiques	1

BOSPHORUS

Nusretiye Camii

İstanbul Modern

Kılıç Ali Paşa Hamamı

Turkish Orthodox Church of Panghia

KARAKÖY

Galataport cruise ship terminal and complex

Karaköy ferry terminal for Haydarpaşa & Kadıköy

Yeralti Camii

TOPHANE

Crimean Memorial Church

Botter House

ŞİŞHANE

Galata Mevlevi Lodge (Galata Mevlevihanesi)

GALİPDEDE CAD

Galata Tower (Galata Kulesi)

GALATA

Tünel (İstiklal)

Kamondo steps

Ottoman Bank Museum/ SALT Gallery

Jewish Museum (500 Yıl Vakfı Türk Musevileri Müzesi)

Church of St Peter and St Paul

Arap Camii

Tünel (Karaköy)

KARAKÖY GALATA

Azar Kapı Camii

GOLDEN HORN

ATATÜRK BRIDGE

Rahmi M. Koç Industrial Museum, Miniatürk & Santralistanbul Energy Museum

N

HALİÇ M

| 0 | metres | 150 |
| 0 | yards | 150 |

The whole of Bankalar Caddesi is lined with fine, European-style nineteenth- and early twentieth-century buildings. Just west of the Ottoman Bank Museum, the **Kamondo steps**, sinuously curved, Art Nouveau-style twin staircases, were commissioned by the wealthy Jewish Kamondo family in 1860. They achieved iconic status in the 1960s when they were photographed by Henri Cartier-Bresson, a friend of equally accomplished Istanbul-Armenian photographer and local resident Ara Güler. Just off Bankalar Caddesi on Galata Kulesi Sokak, the **Church of St Peter and St Paul** dates back to the fifteenth century and still holds Mass every Sunday. Running parallel to Bankalar Caddesi is Galata Mahkamesi Caddesi, where you'll find the **Arap Camii**. Built as a Genoese church, it was converted into a mosque for the Moorish community in the sixteenth century.

Jewish Museum (500 Yil Vakfi Türk Musevileri Müzesi)

MAP P.86, POCKET MAP A16
Büyük Hendek Cad 39 ⓦ muze500.com.
Free, but donations expected.
Originally housed in the Zulfaris synagogue, the Jewish Museum moved to the larger Neve Shalom synagogue in 2015. Celebrating over five hundred years of Sephardic Jewish culture in Istanbul, the museum is split into three main sections: the first chronicles Jewish history in Anatolia from the fourth century BC onwards; the second is largely ethnographic; and the third has a series of touchscreens on Jewish traditions. Also on site are a café, a shop and an associated museum, that of local Jewish artist. For security reasons, you will need your passport or other photo ID for entry.

Istanbul Modern

MAP P.86, POCKET MAP C14
Tophane Iskele Cad 1/1
ⓦ istanbulmodern.org. Charge.
Standing on the same site as the original 2004 gallery, which was housed in a converted period warehouse, the gleaming new Renzo Piano-designed Istanbul Modern opened in 2023. The setting is as grand as the sleek, low-rise steel and glass gallery itself, with fabulous views across the confluence of the Golden Horn and Bosphorus to the Topkapı Palace and old city, and over the Bosphorus to the hills of Asia. Spread over four floors, key features include a rooftop viewing terrace with an eye-catching reflective pool, a second floor devoted to permanent and temporary exhibitions, a fine south-facing restaurant with

Getting to, and around, Galata

Most people coming to Galata from the old city take the T1 tram to the Karaköy stop and walk up into the compact, hillside neighbourhood to see the sights, shop, eat or go to a club. Alternatively, take the nearby late-nineteenth-century underground funicular Tünel (see page 147) to its top, İstiklal station, and walk down. Coming from Taksim Square, the antique tram (see page 147) running down pedestrianized İstiklal Caddesi will save you 1.5km of walking. Coming in from the northern suburbs and Taksim, the M2 metro to Şişhane is useful. All sights and listings in Galata and its immediate environs are best approached in this way, unless otherwise stated, and thence on foot.

Karaköy District

extensive vistas, an arthouse cinema, library and the inevitable shop. There's a good mix of Turkish and international artists on show, with a regularly changing series of temporary exhibitions, as well as a permanent collection themed to outline the development of contemporary Turkish art.

Kılıç Ali Paşa Hamamı

MAP P.86, POCKET MAP C14
Kılıç Ali Paşa Hamamı Hamam Sok 1 📍 1
Tophane ⓦ kilicalipasahamami.com.
Charge.

Attached to the sixteenth-century Kılıç Ali Paşa mosque, on the north side of Galata bridge, this superb Turkish bathhouse opened in 2013 after a seven-year restoration process. Like the mosque, it's the work of Sinan and is a quite beautiful example of an Ottoman-era hamam, with the brickwork of the domed changing room lovingly exposed, light streaming in through small, star-shaped windows in the dome surmounting the bathing areas. Separate times for women and men.

Rahmi M. Koç Industrial Museum

MAP P.86, POCKET MAP D1
Hasköy Cad 5. Buses #47, #47E, #54/HT or
Haliç ferry to Hasköy pier ⓦ rmk-museum.
org.tr. Charge.

The first and best of three worthwhile and, certainly for Istanbul, unusual sights dotted along the north bank of the Golden Horn. Long a shipbuilding area, part of the museum is appropriately housed in what was, in the eighteenth century, a foundry for ships' chains and anchors. Today, it is home to everything from penny-farthings to Royal Enfield motorcycles, Trabants to Rolls-Royces and a working tram to a model railway. Other highlights include a working ship's bridge, complete with echo sounder and alarm, and a street of period shops and houses. It's the largest collection of industrial-era artefacts in Turkey, the vision of a member of one of Turkey's wealthiest families, and contains a couple of upmarket café-restaurants.

Miniatürk

MAP P.86, POCKET MAP D1
İmrahor Cad. Buses #47, #47E or #54/
HT or Haliç ferry to Sütlüce and walk
Ⓦ miniaturk.com.tr. Charge.

Northwest of the Rahmi M. Koç
Industrial Museum, just beyond the
massive Haliç bridge, this attraction
is a great hit with the locals,
displaying a hundred 1:25 scale
models of Turkey's most important
sights. The majority are buildings,
though a couple of geological
wonders – Cappadocia's famed
fairy chimneys and Pamukkale's
travertine terraces – have snuck in.
The models are arranged around
a near 2km-long signed route in
a walled enclosure near the banks
of the Golden Horn. If you're
pressed for time to see the real
thing, here are Istanbul's very own
Süleymaniye Mosque, Dolmabahçe
Palace and Haghia Sophia – there's
even the 1970s Bosphorus Bridge
and Atatürk airport.

Miniatürk

Santralistanbul Energy Museum

MAP P.86, POCKET MAP D1
Kazımkarabekir Cad 2. Free bus from
Taksim Square, buses #54/HT, #99 or Haliç
ferry to Eyüp pier Ⓦ santralistanbul.org.
Free; extra for guided tours.

The furthest of the three Golden
Horn attractions from the city
centre and right at the head of the
inlet, the Energy Museum is housed
in a converted power station that
began life in 1914 and was for
many years the city's sole electricity
producer. The Energy Museum
has carefully preserved the plant's
control room, where a massive
bank of dials, switches and gauges
helped workers keep control of the
giant Siemens engines. Thrown in
for good measure is some far more
cutting-edge technical wizardry,
including a thermal-imaging screen.
The Energy Play Zone is all about
fun meeting science, with 22
interactive exhibits.

GALATA AND THE WATERFRONT DISTRICTS

Shops

Aponia

MAP P.86, POCKET MAP B14
Galipdede Cad 101/a ⓦ aponiastore.com.
For a wide range of original,
quirky yet stylish Istanbul-themed
designer T-shirts and other apparel,
Aponia is the place to come. It's a
tiny store, but the owners pack a
lot of affordable merchandise into a
small space.

Artena

MAP P.86, POCKET MAP A15
Camekan Sok 1. ⓣ 0212 243 5318.
Established in 2004, this
designer boutique stocks a range
of handcrafted jewellery, hats
and bags, plus a range of ethnic
artefacts collected from Anatolian
villages and traditional jewellery
from the southeast. You'll likely
be offered tea or coffee as you
browse.

Crash

MAP P.86, POCKET MAP A14
Galipdede Cad 35. ⓣ 0212 292 4364.

The Galata neo-bohemian's outlet
of choice, this small store stocks
a range of in-house designed
T-shirts and other clothing as well
as carefully chosen (to be slightly
alt and cool) end-of-line jeans,
shorts, tees, hoodies, dresses and
the like – and knocks them out at
fair prices.

Hammam

MAP P.86, POCKET MAP A15
Kule Çıkmazı ⓦ hammam.com.tr.
A wide range of Turkish bath
accessories is on offer here, from
quality cotton *peştemal* wraps
to fancy soap bowls, as well as
handmade soaps and lotions – all
presented with panache.

Hiç Contemporary Crafts

MAP P.86, POCKET MAP B14
Lüleci Hendek Sok 35, Karaköy
ⓦ hiccrafts.com.
This small shop specialises in
tasteful furniture and accessories
by local designers. Most items
have an ethnic feel about
them, though they are very
contemporary in style. Look out

Hiç Contemporary Crafts

also for the fine *ikat* and *suzani* fabrics from Central Asia.

Lale Plak

MAP P.86, POCKET MAP B14
Galipdede Cad 1 ⓦ facebook.com/laleplak1.

Located where Galipdede Caddesi joins throbbing İstiklal Caddesi, Lale Plak is the Istanbul music-buffs' store of choice. It was established over fifty years ago and leafing through the racks of jazz and rock vinyl classics is a retro delight, but there's plenty of Turkish and Western music on CD for sale too.

Sofa Art and Antiques

MAP P.86, POCKET MAP B14
Serdar-ı Ekrem Sok 47, Galata
ⓦ kashifsofa.com.

Established back in 1976 by husband-and-wife team Kaşif and Dilek, Sofa Art and Antiques is situated on very fashionable Serdar-ı Ekrem street, near the Galata Tower. It is a reputable place to hunt down antiques and vintage items both from Europe and Ottoman Turkey, including calligraphy, tiles, miniatures and textiles. There's another branch in the Grand Bazaar.

Cafés

Café Privato

MAP P.86, POCKET MAP A14
Tımarcı Sok 3B, Galata ☎ 0212 293 2055.

This cosy café is well known for its superb fixed-menu breakfast spread. Sit down to enjoy a mouthwatering array of dishes that include homemade organic jams, Georgian pancakes (the owner is of Georgian origin), several different cheeses, dressed olives and much more. One breakfast is generally enough for two people, and there are lots of other options for later in the day. €

Fasuli

MAP P.86, POCKET MAP C14
İskele Cad 10–12 ⓣ 1 Tophane
ⓦ fasuli.com.tr.

White beans in tomato sauce (*kuru fasulye*) are a standard Turkish dish, and here they are an art form. The tender, melt-in-your-mouth beans are grown in the foothills of the Pontic Alps, high above the owners' native Trabzon on the Black Sea, then smothered in a butter-rich tomato sauce. They make for a bargain lunchtime treat, but there's much else to choose from besides. The restaurant, housed in an attractive period building, has a pleasant roof terrace. Unlicensed. €

Galata Konak

MAP P.86, POCKET MAP A15
Haci Ali Sok 2 ⓦ galatakonak.com.tr.

Really two places in one, the ground-floor patisserie is great for a range of quality Turkish and European-style cakes and desserts. Upstairs, reached by the antiquated lift original to this turn-of-the-nineteenth-century building, is a popular roof-terrace restaurant with a range of local and international dishes ranging from *menemen*, a scrambled egg, onion and pepper delight, to pasta dishes. It's especially packed for Sunday brunch. Great views, but unlicensed. €

Karaköy Güllüoğlu

MAP P.86, POCKET MAP B15
Rihtim Cad 17 ⓦ karakoylokantasi.com.

This cavernous place is certainly not the cheapest in the city for *baklava* and other Turkish nut and pastry concoctions, but it's arguably the best. It's invariably packed with locals tucking into walnut- or pistachio-rich *baklava*, which is rich and buttery with a dry texture (cheaper places often skimp on the nuts and overdo the syrup). Often, it comes with a splodge of chewy Maraş ice cream. Unlicensed. €

Restaurants

Galista

MAP P.86, POCKET MAP B14

Şahkulu,Şahkapısı 2, Galata,
Ⓦ galista.com.tr.

Every bit as busy and good as
next door's longer established
Güney, it's hard to get a seat on
occasion, especially weekends
when the weather is fine and
queues for Galata Tower long.
The *mantı* here is excellent, as is
the lentil soup, though they do
everything from tasty omelettes
to shrimp casseroles and a
cheese plate to smoked salmon.
Licenced. €€

Güney

MAP P.86, POCKET MAP A14

Kuledibi Sah Kapısı 6 ☎ 0212 249 0393.

Once a down to earth *lokanta*,
today *Güney* serves a wide
range of traditional Turkish and
international dishes, from kebabs
to pizzas, *pide* to steaks. Standards
remain high, and the interior
is stylish. The location, right
on the square below the tower,
is appealing, though it is often

Ritim Galata

extremely crowded at lunch times
and early evening. Licensed. €€

Karaköy Lokantası

MAP P.86, POCKET MAP C15

Kermankeş Cad 37/A ☎ 0212 292 4455.

Frequented by local office
workers and merchants by day
and a more sophisticated crowd
by night, this is one of the most
atmospheric places to eat in the
city, with its beautiful turquoise-
tiled interior and excellent
waterfront location. The service
and food are top-notch, with
a particularly enticing range of
veggie and seafood starters, fish
of the day, mains and kebabs.
Licensed. €€

Nola Galata

MAP P.86, POCKET MAP A15

Galata Kulesi Sok 10 ☎ 0212 243 1717.

Though located in a historical
area, this place has a contemporary
ambience. There's a small but
decent choice of Turkish and
international dishes (think pizza
and pasta), and if the soup of the
day is chestnut, don't hesitate to
order it. The restaurant also has a
big, beautiful garden. Licenced. €€

Bars

Ritim Galata

MAP P.86, POCKET MAP A15
Galata Kulesi Sok 3/C ☎ 0212 292 4929.
Between the Galata Tower and
Nardis Jazz Club, this laidback
little bar combines a stylish
exposed brick and mezzanine-
floor split interior with mellow
sounds from the DJ and a decent
Turkish and international menu.
There are tables out on the
cobbled street for hot evenings –
and the smokers.

Sensus

MAP P.86, POCKET MAP A15
Büyük Hendek Cad 5, Galata. ☎ 0212 245 5657.
Offering the best choice of
domestically-produced wines in
Istanbul, this cavernous brick-
lined cellar bar is tucked away
down a side street benneath the
Galata Tower. There are set menus
(Turkish and international) on
offer, as well as wine by the glass.
Be warned, it gets ultra-busy on
Friday and Saturday evenings.

The Tower Pub

MAP P.86, POCKET MAP A15
Galata Kulesi Sok 4 ⓦ thetowerpub.com.
This is a Turkish take on an
English pub, complete with TV
screens showing football and you
can play darts. It's hospitable and
laid back, a nice stop on a pub
crawl or a good place to go to
with friends.

Unter

MAP P.86, POCKET MAP C15
Kara Ali Kaptan Sok 4 ⓦ unter.com.tr.
This is the cool, young Istanbulite's
drinking den of choice in hip
Karaköy. But there's more to *Unter*
than mere alcohol, as it prides itself
on a constantly changing menu of
organic dishes, and things pick up
on Thursday, Friday and Saturday
nights, when assorted DJs take
centre stage.

Clubs & venues

Fosil

MAP P.86, POCKET MAP B15
Kermeraltı Caddesi 16/A ☎ 0552 218 0762.
Nowhere is more indicative
of this once gritty dockland
neighbourhood's transformation
to urban hip than this very
cool bar and club, which has
an interior decorated with
exposed piping, bricks and bare
bulbs. The narrow entrance
way leaves you unprepared for
the spectacular views across the
Bosphorus once you're inside.
It gets very busy on Friday and
Saturday nights, despite high
prices for drinks.

Nardis Jazz Club

MAP P.86, POCKET MAP A15
Kuledibi Sok 14 ⓦ nardisjazz.com.
This is one of the most
accessible and intimate jazz clubs
in the city, with the usual roster
of (very talented) Turkish jazz
performers complemented by
a whole host of international
artists. Sets start at 9.30pm, but
later at the weekends. Admission
prices are fairly reasonable,
especially when you consider the
location and that it attracts fans
of all ages. You can expect an
atmospheric bare-brick interior,
as well as a bar-grub-type menu.

Salon IKSV

MAP P.86, POCKET MAP A13
Sadi Konuralp Cad 5, Şişhane
ⓦ saloniksv.com.
This multi-purpose venue
runs under the auspices of
the Istanbul Foundation for
Culture and Arts (IKSV). It
attracts and hosts a wide-range
of performers, from electronic
music to jazz and indie rock to
traditional world. There's a cool
upstairs terrace bar and theatre
hall, and admission prices are
usually very reasonable.

Beyoğlu and Taksim

Draped across the hilltop above Galata is Beyoğlu, the frenetic entertainment quarter of the metropolis. Heart of the action is 1.5-km-long İstiklal Caddesi (Independence Street), running from the upper Tünel station north to bland but impressively vast Taksim Square. From the seventeenth century onwards this became the European quarter of the city, home to the palatial residences of foreign merchants, ambassadors and members of the city's Greek and Armenian communities. Typically late nineteenth-century Neoclassical, Art Nouveau and Secessionist-style apartment blocks line the streets, punctuated by grand consular buildings, churches and period arcades. Beneath their grand facades, Istanbulites and foreign visitors shop, visit a gallery, take in a film, head up to a rooftop bar to watch the sun sink over the old city across the water and while away the night at a trendy club or live music venue.

İstiklal Caddesi: Tünel to Galatasaray Meydani

MAP P.96, POCKET MAP B13–D11

Leaving the upper İstiklal Tünel station and following the antique tramline round onto İstiklal Caddesi, the first sight of interest is the beautiful curvilinear Art Nouveau facade of the **Botter House**, built in 1901 by Italian architect D'Aronco for the Dutch tailor to Sultan Abdülhamit II. A little way beyond, best reached by heading down steep Kumbaracı Sokak, the pretty Anglican **Crimean Memorial Church** or Christ Church was constructed in 1868 to commemorate those who fell in the Crimean War. The architect was G.E. Street, also responsible for the Royal Courts of Justice in London. It's attractively set in a green, walled compound, and visitors are requested to leave a donation, but it's not always open – try a Sunday morning service. Further up on the right, steps lead down to **St Mary Draperis**,

a Catholic church designed by Semprini in 1904 on the site of a 1678 original.

On the opposite side of the street, the defunct **Patisserie Markiz**, still advertised by gold-leaf lettering on the glass, has a stunning **fin-de-siècle** interior with a pair of faïence tile wall panels, Le Printemps and L'Automne, imported from France. Closed for some years, its future is uncertain. Just north of Markiz is a pretty nineteenth-century arcade, Cite de Syrie (see page 99). Opposite the arcade is the **Borusan Arts & Cultural Centre** (İstiklal Cad 213, ⓦ borusansanat.com), which is home to one of Turkey's leading private orchestras and an art gallery. Continuing up İstiklal on the right is the impressive Dutch consulate, the **Palais de Hollande**, built in Neoclassical style in 1858. On the same side further up the **Merkez Han**, owned by Koç University, houses the Research Centre for Anatolian Studies, which has regular free

Crimea Memorial Church

exhibitions of an archeological and historical nature. Back on the right, set back from the road, is the very attractive **St Anthoine** Franciscan church with a red-brick Neogothic facade, built in 1913 on the site of a much earlier church.

Meşrutiyet Caddesi

MAP P.96, POCKET MAP A13–B12

Running parallel to İstiklal Caddesi to the west and easily reached by cutting through one of the alleys joining them, this busy street is home to yet more fine turn-of-the-nineteenth-century buildings as well as a smattering of restaurants such as *Mikla* (see page 107), and the **fin-de-siècle** *Büyük Londra* hotel (see page 138) and its wonderful period bar (see page 108). At the north end of the street, where it joins Hamalbaşı Caddesi, is the grandiose, Renaissance-style **British Consulate**, built in 1855.

Getting to, and around, İstiklal Caddesi (Beyoğlu)

You can reach İstiklal Caddesi from the old city on the T1 tram to Karaköy and then either walk up the hill or take the Tünel funicular (see page 147) to the southern end of the street. Alternatively, use the M2 metro to Şişhane or Taksim. For the north Taksim end, it's possible to ride the T1 tram to Kabataş, then the F1 funicular to Taksim Square. Wherever you start, explorations are best done on foot, though judicious use of the antique tram that runs the whole length of the street, stopping at points en route (see page 147), is fun. From the northern suburbs, you can use the M2 metro to Taksim at the north end of İstiklal Caddesi, or Şişhane at the south end. Unless otherwise stated, these will be the best ways to visit the sights and venues in this chapter.

Beyoğlu & Taksim

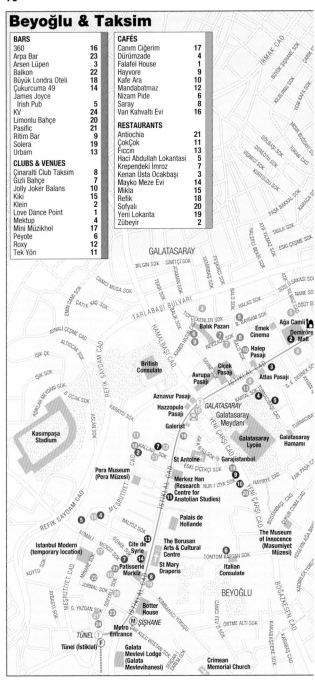

BARS

360	16
Arpa Bar	23
Arsen Lüpen	3
Balkon	22
Büyük Londra Oteli	18
Çukurcuma 49	14
James Joyce Irish Pub	5
KV	24
Limonlu Bahçe	20
Pasific	21
Ritim Bar	9
Solera	19
Urbam	13

CLUBS & VENUES

Çinaralti Club Taksim	8
Gizli Bahçe	7
Jolly Joker Balans	10
Kiki	15
Klein	2
Love Dance Point	1
Mektup	4
Mini Müzikhol	17
Peyote	6
Roxy	12
Tek Yön	11

CAFÉS

Canım Ciğerim	17
Dürümzade	4
Falafel House	1
Hayvore	9
Kafe Ara	10
Mandabatmaz	12
Nizam Pide	6
Saray	8
Van Kahvaltı Evi	16

RESTAURANTS

Antiochia	21
ÇokÇok	11
Ficcın	13
Haci Abdullah Lokantasi	5
Krependeki Imroz	7
Kenan Usta Ocakbaşı	3
Mayko Meze Evi	14
Mikla	15
Refik	18
Sofyalı	20
Yeni Lokanta	19
Zübeyir	2

ACCOMMODATION

Büyük Londra	2
Devman	7
Divan Taksim Suites	1
Marmara Pera	4
Pera Palace	5
Richmond Hotel	8
Tom Tom Suites	6
Villa Zurich	3

SHOPS

Ada Books	13
Ambar	7
Berrin Akyüz	12
By Retro	14
Demirören Mall	1
Homer	9
Kontra Plak	10
Leila Boutique	9
Mavi	11
Mephisto	3
Mor Taki	4
Roll	5
Tarihi Meşhur Beyoğlu Çikolatacısı	1
The Works	6
Vakko	2

Architect Charles Barry was also responsible for London's Houses of Parliament, but unfortunately today his work is semi-obscured by massive compound walls built after a terrorist bomb attack in 2003.

Pera Palace Hotel

MAP P.96, POCKET MAP A13
Meşrutiyet Cad 52 Ⓦ perapalace.com.

The most famous building on Meşrutiyet Caddesi, this grand hotel was completed in 1892 to accommodate gentry arriving in "Stamboul" on the trans-European Orient Express (see page 144). The architect was the prolific Frenchman Alexander Vallaury, also responsible for the Neoclassical Archeology Museum across in the old city (see page 42) and the Ottoman Bank down in Galata (see page 85). After years of neglect, it has been restored to its former glory, a necessary process that has resulted in a loss of some of its former character and a steep rise in prices, but nostalgia buffs will be tempted to take afternoon tea and cake in the elegant ground-floor **tea rooms** and conjure up the shenanigans of past guests. These have included Greto Garbo and

Zsa Zsa Gabor, Ernest Hemingway, Alfred Hitchcock and Atatürk, the founder of the Turkish Republic (the room he regularly used, 401, is a museum). The notorious spy Mata Hari also stayed here and, last but not least, another regular, Agatha Christie, wrote *Murder on the Orient Express* in her favoured room, 411.

Pera Museum (Pera Müzesi)

MAP P.96, POCKET MAP A13
Meşrutiyet Cad 65 Ⓦ peramuseum.org.
Charge.

As much an art gallery as a museum, the *Pera Museum* is housed in a beautifully restored late nineteenth-century building that was originally the prestigious *Bristol Hotel* – once a rival to the nearby *Pera Palace* and *Büyük Londra* hotels. On the first floor is a permanent exhibition of Kütahya tiles, similar to the more famous İznik ware, alongside a collection of surprisingly interesting weights and measures from across the ages. On the second floor are the works of Orientalist painters from the seventeenth to nineteenth centuries, the most striking (and

Nevizade Sokak

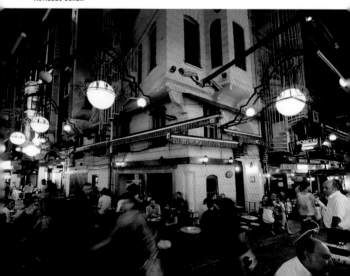

A passage to Europe

One of the delights of exploring İstiklal Caddesi and its offshoots is its nineteenth-century arcades. These attractive covered passages (*pasaj* in Turkish) are redolent of an era when Beyoğlu was Pera, İstiklal Caddesi the Grand Rue de Pera and the area home to a cosmopolitan mix of Armenians, Jews, Greeks and foreign residents. By far the best known and touristy is the **Cite de Pera**, more commonly known by its Turkish name **Çiçek Pasajı** (Flower Arcade), just north of Galatasaray Meydanı. Beautifully restored and today full of overpriced restaurants, its name derives from the White Russian émigrés who sold flowers here in the 1920s. The **Cite de Syrie** (Suriye Pasajı in Turkish), at the southern end of İstiklal Caddesi, was designed by a Greek architect in 1908 and has an ornate facade as well as housing the vintage clothing store *By Retro* (see page 102). Perhaps the most attractive of them all, however, is the **Passage d'Europe (Avrupa Pasajı)**, which links Meşrutiyet Caddesi with Sahane Sok. Three storeys high, with a barrel-vaulted glazed roof and lined with Neoclassical statues, each of which represents a different craft, it's home today to some fine antique and souvenir shops. Other historic arcades include **Hazzopulo**, **Aznavur**, **Halep** (Aleppo) and **Atlas** pasajıs.

valuable) of which is Osman Hamdi's *Tortoise Trainer*, brought back to its native land from abroad for a cool $3.5 million in 2004. Floors three, four and five are devoted to temporary exhibitions, and frequently feature well-known artists. There's also a very decent café and shop.

Nevizade Sokak

MAP P.96, POCKET MAP B11

This narrow pedestrian alley, running parallel to İstiklal Caddesi behind Çiçek Pasajı (see box, page 99), is arguably the liveliest in the whole city. Lined by restaurants and bars, all with tables spilling out into the alleyway, it's worth fighting your way down just for the atmosphere or, even better, to join the raucous diners in a traditional *meyhane* (tavern) such as *İmroz* (see page 106).

Galatasaray Meydanı

MAP P.96, POCKET MAP B12

This small square about halfway along İstiklal Caddesi is a stop for the antique tram. It's named after prestigious **Galatasaray Lycée** on the south side of the square, a school dating back to 1481, though the current building was erected in 1908. Students here formed one of Turkey's leading football clubs, Galatasaray, in 1905, and there's a small **museum** to the club in the restored Neoclassical building opposite. Hidden away below the square to the southeast is uber-cool **Garajistanbul** (Kaymakan Reşit Bey Sok 11, off Yeniçarşı Caddesi, ☎0212 244 4499), which stands as Istanbul's leading avant-garde performing arts and music venue.

Çukurcuma and Cihangir

MAP P.96, POCKET MAP C13 & E11

The warren of streets south and east of the northern section of İstiklal Caddesi make up the districts of Çukurcuma and Cihangir. The former is home to the fascinating **Museum of Innocence** and boasts a welter of bric-a-brac shops and vintage/alternative clothing

Vintage furnitures at Çukurcuma

outlets – especially on Turnacıbaşı Sokak. This steep, twisting street is also known for its famous Turkish baths, the **Galatasaray Hamamı** (Turnacı Başı Sok 24, Ⓦ galatasarayhamami.com) which date back to 1481. Cihangir is one of the aspiring urban bohemian's abode of choice in Istanbul, and has a number of trendy café-bars and shops.

The Museum of Innocence (Masumiyet Müzesi)

MAP P.96, POCKET MAP C13

Çukurcuma Cad 24 Ⓦ masumiyetmuzesi. org. Charge, extra for audio guide.

Although it can be visited as a stand-alone attraction, it is best visiting if you've read the eponymous book by Turkey's Nobel Prize-winning author, Istanbulite Orhan Pamuk. In the book, the obsessive upper-class Kemal collects everyday items touched by his object of desire, an unsuitable young woman from an impoverished background. The objects are displayed as they were acquired, starting with over 4000 cigarette butts. The sequence finishes on the top floor with the bed where Kemal lays dying at the close of the novel.

İstiklal Caddesi: Galatasaray Meydan to Taksim

MAP P.96, POCKET MAP B12–D11

Although still lined by mainly grand nineteenth-century apartment blocks, İstiklal Caddesi becomes increasingly mainstream, period arcades apart (see page 99), as you approach Taksim Square. There are a number of **cinemas** here showing foreign films (see page 148) including the **Atlas** at İstiklal Cad 129 and further up on the left, the multiplex **Cinemaximum Fitaş** at no. 24–26. Also on the left is the Demirören shopping mall (see page 102) and, not far beyond it, the whitewashed **Ağa Camii** (1596), the only mosque on the street. A little way past the Fitaş cinema is the **Akbanksanat** (İstiklal Cad 8/A Ⓦ akbanksanat. com), a culture and arts centre with exhibitions, a dance studio, theatre, cinema and café. Opposite is **Aya Triada**, a monumental Greek Orthodox church built in 1880.

Taksim Square (Taksim Meydanı)

MAP P.96, POCKET MAP D10

Live music at Babylon

Istanbul's leading music venue (Birahane Sok 1, Ⓦ babylon.com. tr) has been living up to its "Babylon turns Istanbul on" motto for years – especially after its recent move out to a hip new venue, a refurbished former brewery in Bomonti. Acts include everything from world music bands to Turkish fusion. Get tickets for live music direct or via Biletix (Ⓦ biletix.com).

Massive Taksim Square has little to recommend it bar its role as transport hub, but it has come to symbolize the secular identity of the Turkish Republic. It has long been a focal point for protests and in 2013 an occupy Wall Street type demonstration, protesting the destruction of a green area of the square, Gezi Park, brought Taksim to TV screens worldwide. Taksim Square takes its name from a reservoir built in 1732 (*taksim* means distribution) to distribute water through the city.

Military Museum (Asker Müzesi)

MAP P.96, POCKET MAP D10
Valikonağı Cad, Harbiye Ⓜ 2 Osmanbey
☎ 0212 233 2720. Charge.

A fifteen-minute walk north of Taksim Square along busy Cumhüriyet Caddesi, this interesting museum traces the history of Turkish warfare and weaponry from the origins of the Turks in Central Asia through to the intervention of the Turkish Republic in Cyprus in 1974. Most exhibits are staidly displayed in dark-wood glass-fronted cabinets, but it's easy to while away an hour or two looking at everything from a huge section of the chain used to block the Golden Horn in the Byzantine era to heavy machine guns used in the Turkish defence of Gallipoli in 1915, and the embroidered tents used by campaigning sultans to a superb collection of Ottoman armour and weaponry. The **Mehter Band**, who accompanied the Ottoman war machine into battle from 1289 onwards, play rousing martial music on the first floor between 3 and 4pm each afternoon.

Asker Müzesi

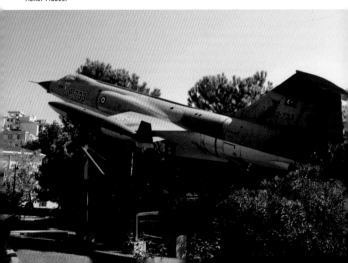

Shops

Ada Books

MAP P.96, POCKET MAP B13
İstiklal Cad 20. ⓦ facebook.com/
istiklalada.

Stocks a decent range of glossy titles on Istanbul and Turkey along with CDs, DVDs and magazines; always busy because of its well-regarded (licensed) café-restaurant.

Ambar

MAP P.96, POCKET MAP B12
Kallavi Sok 12, off İstiklal Cad.

A family business concentrating on organic and whole foods, as well as natural soaps and lotions.

Berrin Akyüz

MAP P.96, POCKET MAP D13
Akarsu Yokuşu 22.

Situated in trendy Cihangir, this small boutique is a treasure-trove of one-off fashion and home accessory objects, from sheep-shaped knitted bags to cushion covers, felt jewellery and silk scarves.

By Retro

MAP P.96, POCKET MAP B13
Suriye Pasajı, off İstiklal Cad.

A veritable cornucopia, hidden away in the basement of this historic arcade. Owner Hakan trawls Europe for vintage and retro clothing and decorative household items such as old phones and radios.

Demirören Mall

MAP P.96, POCKET MAP C11
İstiklal Cad. ⓦ facebook.com/
demirorenistiklal.

With so many high-street stores and historic shopping passages, it's hard to see why İstiklal Caddesi needed a mall, but if you're in search of Gap, Mothercare or even a Turkish fashion giant like Vakko (see page 103) this accessible location means you don't have to head into the suburbs to find them. Also houses a good cinema.

Homer

MAP P.96, POCKET MAP B12
Yeni Çarşı Cad 28 ⓦ homerbooks.com.

Great bookshop tucked away just off İstiklal Caddesi with a superb range of Turkey-related material – art, archeology, literature and politics as well as specialist books on many other subjects – it even has a good children's section.

Kontra Plak

MAP P.96, POCKET MAP B12
Kontra Plak Yeni Çarşı Cad 60/A,
Galatasaray ⓦ kontrarecords.com.

This hip basement record store caters to cool young Istanbulites and the youthful expats who have made this neighbourhood their own. Browse through an impressive range of records and CDs of all genres, from Turkey and beyond.

Leila Boutique

MAP P.96, POCKET MAP C12
Altıpatlar Sok 6 ⓦ leilaconceptstore.com.

Leila Boutique has amassed a fine collection of vintage clothes – from the nineteenth century to the 1960s – as well as cushion-covers, throws and the like.

Mavi

MAP P.96, POCKET MAP B12
İstiklal Cad 189/A.

Mavi is well known in Turkey for its quality denim goods and other clothing, and if you're after a non-crass souvenir T-shirt, its ever-changing and witty range of Istanbul-inspired designs is worth checking out.

Mephisto

MAP P.96, POCKET MAP C11
Istiklal Cad 125, Beyoğlu
ⓦ mephisto.com.tr.

This modern book and music store stocks a good range of Turkish music CDs and is popular with young Istanbulites who head to its pleasant café to escape the throngs on the main shopping street outside.

Mavi

Mor Taki

MAP P.96, POCKET MAP C12
Turnacıbaşı Sok 10B, off İstiklal Cad
📞 0212 292 8817.
At the İstiklal Caddesi end of this
trendy street, this chic, hole-in-
the-wall outlet is worth a look for
its range of alternative, handmade
jewellery.

Roll

MAP P.96, POCKET MAP C12
Turnacıbaşı 38/1, off İstiklal Cad.
In a grubby passage full of
grungy alternative clothes stalls,
this one stands out for its funny
line of T-shirts inspired by
Turkey's recent past, from iconic
Turkish film characters to the
logos of so-bad-they're-good
Turkish cars.

Tarihi Meşhur Beyoğlu Çikolatacısı

MAP P.96, POCKET MAP C11
İstiklal Cad 69/A.
Istanbulites love their *baklava*
and traditional desserts, but
they also have a passion for
chocolate. Buy almond, hazelnut
or pistachio slabs of the stuff
from this chocolatier.

The Works

MAP P.96, POCKET MAP C12
Faik Paşa Sok 6.
A muddle of retro delights awaits
the visitor here, from tin toys
to vintage Pepsi bottles and the
chrome hood mascots of 1950s
American cars. It supplied the
nearby Museum of Innocence (see
page 100) with some exhibits.

Vakko

MAP P.96, POCKET MAP C11
Demirören Mall, İstiklal Cad.
For a Turkish take on
mainstream fashion for both
men and women, *Vakko* is a
reliable choice – the fact it's
been in business over fifty years
speaks volumes about its quality
materials and timeless designs.

Cafés

Canım Ciğerim

MAP P.96, POCKET MAP A13
Minare Sok 1 🌐 canimcigerim.com.
Just off lively Asmalımescit, "My
Dearest Liver" specializes in skewers
of small cubes of the tenderest liver
imaginable, dished up with salad

Kafe Ara

and fresh flatbread. Non-offal-eaters may prefer the chicken or lamb options. Unlicensed. €

Dürümzade

MAP P.96, POCKET MAP B11
Kamer Hatun Cad 26/A Ⓦ durumzade-restaurant.business.site.
If you want to sit and linger, forget this place. But if you want to try a *dürüm* (wrap) filled with the most succulent chargrilled meat for a bargain price, then *Dürümzade* is for you. One of the secrets employed here is to get the very best, slightly chewy flatbread, rub it with a subtle blend of spices and toast it on the grill before adding the meat filling. €

Falafel House

MAP P.96, POCKET MAP D10
Şehit Muhtar Cad 19, off Taksim Square
Ⓦ falafelhouse.com.tr.
Many Turkey first-timers assume Middle Eastern street food like *hummus* and falafel will be staples here too, but they're not. That's why this cheap and cheerful Palestinian-run place is such a great find. The decor is greasy spoon, but there are a few tables out on

the street for people-watching. Unlicensed. €

Hayvore

MAP P.96, POCKET MAP C12
Turnacıbaşı Sok 4, off İstiklal Cad
Ⓦ hayvore.com.tr.
Pick from a wide range of steamtray dishes in this authentic, eastern Black Sea restaurant – there's the inevitable corn bread to mop up the juices from delectable chickpea or white bean stews, or to accompany the excellent cabbage soup. Unlicensed. €

Kafe Ara

MAP P.96, POCKET MAP B12
Tosbağı Sok 8/A, off Yeniçarşı Cad Ⓣ 0212 245 4105.
Owned by Turkey's leading photographer, Armenian-Istanbulite Ara Güler, this sophisticated café is adorned with marvellous black and white images of his city. Mix of Turkish and international dishes. Unlicensed. €

Mandabatmaz

MAP P.96, POCKET MAP B12
Olivia Geçidi, off İstiklal Cad
Ⓦ mandabatmaz.com.tr.

Having been superseded by tea as the national drink, Turkish coffee is not always as great as it would like to be. However, this tiny coffee joint is an exception, and you can sip a rich, velvet brew as good as you'll find anywhere in the Middle East. It's been going since 1967, but has remained resolutely unchanged since, with customers sitting on low stools in the cramped interior or out in the alley. €

Nizam Pide

MAP P.96, POCKET MAP C11
Büyükparmakkapı Sok 18, off İstiklal Cad Ⓦ nizampide.com.
Pide is often described as Turkish pizza, but it's actually quite different. Essentially a large, oval semi-leavened flatbread baked in a wood oven with a variety of toppings – standards are cheddar-like *kaşarlı* cheese, chopped-meat *kuşbaşı* or *beyaz peynirli* – goat's cheese and parsley. This is a great place to try it. Unlicensed. €

Saray

MAP P.96, POCKET MAP C11
İstiklal Cad 107 ☎ 0212 292 3434.
This popular place, spread over several floors, does main meals, but is best known for its splendid traditional desserts, from *tavuk göğüsü* (a milk pudding enhanced with semolina and chicken breast) to *fırın sutlaç* (oven-baked rice pudding). Unlicensed. €

Van Kahvaltı Evi

MAP P.96, POCKET MAP D13
Van Kahvaltı Evi Defterdar Yokuşu 52/A, Cihangir ☎ 0212 293 6437.
This all-day breakfast place brings the cuisine of far-flung Van, a predominantly Kurdish city in eastern Turkey, to Istanbul. As well as Turkish standards like olives and cheeses, you can try *kavut* (roasted wheat flour blended with honey and walnuts), *jajı* (yoghurt and cottage cheese) and clotted cream with honey. Extremely busy weekend mornings/lunchtimes. €

Restaurants

Antiochia

MAP P.96, POCKET MAP A13
General Yazgan Sok 3, Asmalımescit Ⓦ antiochiaconcept.com.
Owner Lale Balcı has written about the unique cuisine of her native Hatay, close to the Syrian border, and she and her chefs certainly know how to prepare it. Kebabs done Hatay-style are juicier and spicier than the standard issue, but the real pull is the tasty meze, including the thyme salad *zahter* and spicy hot *muammara*, a walnut and hot pepper dip. Licensed. €€

ÇokÇok

MAP P.96, POCKET MAP B12
Meşrutiyet Cad 51 Ⓦ cokcok.com.tr.
If you can't survive Istanbul without a Thai fix, this is a worthy option, with a Thai chef, the freshest ingredients and stylish surroundings. Best option is the lunchtime special, but the good choice of cocktails is a bonus for a "night-out" feast. €

Hacı Abdullah Lokantası

BEYOĞLU AND TAKSIM

Fıccın

MAP P.96, POCKET MAP B12
Kallavi Sok 13, off İstiklal Cad ☎ 0212
293 3786.

Not the most sophisticated place
in Beyoğlu, but nicely located
down a quiet alley with street tables
and great value for Caucasus-style
dishes such as the eponymous
ficcin, a tasty meat pie; rocket
soup; and the yoghurt-drenched
Caucasian ravioli, *Çerkez mantısı*.
Licensed. €

Haci Abdullah Lokantasi

MAP P.96, POCKET MAP C11
Sakızağacı Cad 17, off İstiklal Cad
Ⓦ haciabdullah.com.tr.

A Beyoğlu institution that's been
serving traditional Turkish fare
(soups, steamtray dishes, grills, pies
and desserts) since 1888. It's right
by the Ağa Camii (see page 100)
so there's no alcohol, and it does
trade on its reputation, so it's not

the cheapest; but the food is good
and the period ambience suitably
sedate. €

Krependeki İmroz

MAP P.96, POCKET MAP B11
Nevizade Sok 24, off İstiklal Cad ☎ 0212
249 9073.

This perennially popular *meyhane*
has been in business since 1941,
and makes the perfect choice for
a memorable *rakı* and fish-fuelled
night out – eat, drink, talk (if
you can make yourself heard over
the other diners) and relax as
you watch the almost constant
procession of revellers parading
by. €€

Kenan Üsta Ocakbaşı

MAP P.96, POCKET MAP D11
Kurabiye Sok 18, off İstiklal Cad
Ⓦ kenanusta.com.tr.

This place is a real treat for all
carnivores, as the master-chef here

Kenan Usta Ocakbaşı

has been grilling choice cuts of meat over charcoal for over forty years. The meze are all freshly prepared to order, and the kebabs and other meat are served up with piles of thin, unleavened bread (*lavaş*), deftly wiped across the grill and smeared with oil and spices. There are tables out on the street if you'd rather dine outside, and it's licensed. €€

Mayko Meze Evi

MAP P.96, POCKET MAP C12
Altıpatlar Sok 2, Cukurcuma
Ⓦ maykomezeevi.business.site.
Specialising in meze dishes, ranging from the fiery yoghurt and ultra-hot chilli *atom* to creamy broad bean dip *fava*, as well as simple grilled fish mains, this tiny back street place has a loyal local clientele, a cool stripped brick interior and an intimate ambience. For hip Çukurcuma, prices are reasonable too. Licenced. €€

Mikla

MAP P.96, POCKET MAP A13
Marmara Pera Hotel, Meşrutiyet Cad 167/185 Ⓦ miklarestaurant.com.
Seventeen floors up on the roof of the towering *Marmara Pera Hotel* (see page 138) this restaurant has sensational views over the old city and Bosphorus as well as excellent food – Turkish/Mediterranean with a Scandinavian twist. Most diners go for the fixed menu, though you can eat a la carte and drink wine by the glass. It's expensive, but worth it for the ambience and views – dress up a bit for this one. €€€€

Refik

MAP P.96, POCKET MAP A13
Sofyalı Sok 10–12, off İstiklal Cad Ⓣ 0212 243 2834.
A low-key place in a busy alley, this intellectual take on the *meyhane* has a good range of meze – including some Black Sea specialities – and the usual grilled fish and meat mains. The set menu is good value if you're in the drinking mood as

all local drinks are included in the price. €€

Sofyalı

MAP P.96, POCKET MAP A13
Sofyalı Sok 9, off İstiklal Cad
Ⓦ sofyali.com.tr.
A sophisticated *meyhane* with a soothing interior, all white walls, stripped wood floors and antique furniture, this busy place is in heavy demand so best to book ahead – especially for Friday and Saturday evenings and for the outside tables. The meze are particularly good, with meat mains and fish on request. Also has a good range of wines and *rakı*. €€

Yeni Lokanta

MAP P.96, POCKET MAP B13
Kumbaracı Yokuşu 66 Ⓦ yenilokanta.com.
Owner/chef Çivan Er was the innovative cook at the famous *Changa* restaurant before opening his own place at the head of this steep alley. Here he concentrates on traditional Anatolian and southeastern Turkish favourites, but gives them a few novel tweaks. For a restaurant that brings droves of well-heeled Istanbulites in from wealthy suburbs, it's reasonably priced, and both the cocktail and wine lists are sound. Advance reservations essential. €€€€

Zübeyir

MAP P.96, POCKET MAP C11
Bekar Sok 28 Ⓦ zubeyirocakbasi.com.tr.
This little place is located at the heart of the Beyoğlu district. Choose a seat around the open charcoal grill and watch your food being made – very pleasant when it's cold, slightly less so when it's the middle of summer. €€

Bars

360

MAP P.96, POCKET MAP B12
Mısır Apartmanı 311, İstiklal Cad Ⓣ 0212 251 1042.

Büyük Londra Oteli

The top floor of this fine nineteenth-century apartment block is home to the upmarket *360* bar-restaurant. Take the lift – and if suitably attired – you can enjoy the 360° views and sip a drink whose price reflects the grandeur of the vista.

Arpa Bar

MAP P.96, POCKET MAP A13
General Yazgan Sok 5 ☎ 0212 249 0550.
This small, corner-plot bar has a very pleasant bare-brick interior, jazz soundtrack and reasonably-priced beers. It's a good choice for a quiet drink in bustling Asmalımescit.

Arsen Lüpen

MAP P.96, POCKET MAP C11
Mis Sok 15 ☎ 0532 676 3943.
A two-floor rustic bar with a dance floor on the bottom floor and a terrace with a wonderful view upstairs. On weekends they play live music – folk, jazz, rock and one day a week there is a Spoken Word night when artists read out their latest pieces or sing their own songs (travelling writers are welcome too). The bar is tricky to find, so you might need to ask around.

Balkon

MAP P.96, POCKET MAP A13
Sehbender Sok 5, Asmalı Mescit
ⓦ balkonbeyoglu.com.
One of Istanbul's most popular rooftop bars – and deservedly so. A mixed Turkish and international menu and wide range of drinks at value for money prices, great views and an ever-changing atmosphere as this place keeps going from breakfast time through to the early hours. DJ sets are standard but live music – from jazz to blues and beyond – also feature.

Büyük Londra Oteli

MAP P.96, POCKET MAP B12
Meşrutiyet Cad 117 ☎ 0212 245 0670.
The bar of this hotel (see page 138), little changed since it first opened in the late nineteenth century to serve drinks to guests arriving on the *Orient Express*, is all dark wood, gilt and antique

furnishings – there's even a parrot in a suitably ornate cage. Take the antiquated lift up to the fine roof bar in warm weather.

Çukurcuma 49

MAP P.96, POCKET MAP C12
Turnacıbaşı Sok 49/A ☎ 0212 249 0048.

This split-level bar-cum-pizzeria based in a former office building is a suitably fashionable hangout for the trendy neighbourhood of Çukurcuma. Exposed brick walls and lots of natural materials give it the homely atmosphere that attracts locals and the district's expat community in equal numbers – that, and the good-value wines from the Aegean Turkish island of Bozcaada.

James Joyce Irish Pub

MAP P.96, POCKET MAP B11
Irish Centre, Balo Sok 26
Ⓦ facebook.com/irishpubthejamesjoyce.

Situated in one of the very liveliest parts of Beyoğlu, this rambling place gets packed to bursting point for big-screen sports events and when there's a band on (most evenings). There's a wide range of continental lagers, local beers and Guinness.

KV

MAP P.96, POCKET MAP A13
Tünel Gecidi 6, off İstiklal Cad ☎ 0212 251 4338.

Sophisticated place at the Asmalımescit entrance to the very pretty nineteenth-century Tünel passage, good in summer when you can sit at outside tables in the potted plant-lined passageway and enjoy a decent glass of wine and a light meal.

Limonlu Bahçe

MAP P.96, POCKET MAP B12
Yeniçarşı Cad 74
Ⓦ limonlubahcebeyoglu.com.

A short stroll downhill from bustling İstiklal Caddesi, this is well worth seeking out for its spacious garden scattered with potted lemon

and other trees, bar grub and decently priced beers and cocktails.

Pasific

MAP P.96, POCKET MAP B13
Sofyalı Sok 4, off Asmalımescit ☎ 0212 292 7642.

Cheap bar on a narrow, busy alley, a good bet for an early beer or two, though they also draw in punters with cheap shot deals. The soundtrack is generally rock, the vibe studenty, the flat-screen TV permanently tuned to Akılı TV – a channel devoted to amusing mishaps from around the world.

Ritim Bar

MAP P.96, POCKET MAP B11
Sahane Sok 20, Balık Pazarı ☎ 0539 859 0095.

No-frills bar attracting a mix of locals and visitors with reasonably priced drinks – the owner also runs the popular *World House Hostel* (see page 138). Really gets going on summer weekends when the party-minded pack the rooftop to dance to a mix of favourite dance sounds.

Solera

MAP P.96, POCKET MAP B12
Yeniçarşı Cad 44, Galatasaray
Ⓦ facebook.com/solerawinery.

Wine bars are few and far between in Istanbul, so to come across this one serving over 1000 Turkish and international wines is a near miracle – especially when the prices are reasonable too. The wine is best enjoyed with one of owner Suleyman Er's meze sampler plates.

Urban

MAP P.96, POCKET MAP C12
Kartal Sok 6. ☎ 0212 252 1325.

Laid-back café-bar on a quiet side street shaded by ivy and dotted with pot plants. There's a wide range of well-priced beers and wine by the glass, as well as a decent selection of salads, sandwiches,

Kiki

pizzas and grills. Chill on the street in summer, or enjoy the hip interior in winter.

Clubs & venues

Çinaraltı Club Taksim

MAP P.96, POCKET MAP B11
Balo Sok 14 ☏ 0542 721 8090.
A two-floor club with a pleasant atmosphere and good music.

Gizli Bahçe

MAP P.96, POCKET MAP B11
Nevizade Sok 15 Ⓦ gizli.business.site.
This upstairs club provides a chilled contrast to the mayhem of Nevizade Sokak (see page 99) below. Lounge on sofas or watch the action below from a balcony listening to an eclectic mix of dance, soul, blues and jazz.

Jolly Joker Balans

MAP P.96, POCKET MAP C11
Balo Sok 22 ☏ 0212 249 0749.
Pub style decor, but very much a music venue, with everything from rock and indie to mainstream pop and dance, this place attracts an eclectic crowd of Istanbulites and visitors. Pub grub and a wide range of drinks available.

Kiki

MAP P.96, POCKET MAP D12
Siraselviler Cad 42 Ⓦ kiki.com.tr.
There's no Bosphorus bling down at understated *Kiki*, a cool club that attracts a younger crowd who go for the deep house DJs. The club is spread over three floors and is best in summer on the roof terrace. Drinks are pricey, but entry is free.

Klein

MAP P.96, POCKET MAP D10
Harbiye Cumhüriyet Cad 4 ☏ 0212 291 8440.
Slightly inconveniently located a kilometre north of Taksim Square, this is the subterranean venue of choice for young, stylish and largely black-clad Istanbul youths seeking like-minded souls, electronica and trendy drinks served from two long bars.

Love Dance Point

MAP P.96, POCKET MAP D10
Cumhüriyet Cad 349 Ⓜ 2 Osmanbey
Ⓦ lovedp.net.

Long-running gay club in this prosperous suburb north of Taksim Square, opposite the Military Museum (see page 101), it makes a gentle introduction to the city's gay scene. The music is pop/dance, both domestic and international.

Mektup

MAP P.96, POCKET MAP C11
İmam Adnan Sok 20, off İstiklal Cad
Ⓦ mektupbar.com.

Even young, hip Istanbulites have great respect for traditional Turkish music, and *Mektup* offers this (Türkü) to a very high standard – it has seen sets by notable artists such as Ebru Destan and Tuğbay Özay. Booking is advisable, especially at weekends.

Mini Müzikhol

MAP P.96, POCKET MAP D12
Soğancı Sok 7, off Sıraselviler Cad
Ⓦ minimuzikhol.club.

The artfully contrived interior and urbane clientele make this one of the best music venues if you're into sophisticated dance and electronica, especially as it attracts a regular supply of well-known international (and local) DJs.

Mini Müzikhol

Peyote

MAP P.96, POCKET MAP B11
Kameriye Sok 4 Ⓦ peyote.com.tr.

This is the best place in the city for alternative music, with electronica on the first floor, live bands on the second and an attractive roof terrace where a mixed bag of musical genres are spun.

Roxy

MAP P.96, POCKET MAP D12
Aslanyatağı Sok 1/3 Ⓦ roxy.com.tr.

Well-established club a little off the main Beyoğlu circuit, *Roxy* mixes contemporary Turkish music and live acts with foreign singers and bands (Marc Almond and Ben Harper have played here). Electronica, rock, blues and world music all feature, playing to a well-heeled Istanbulite crowd.

Tek Yön

MAP P.96, POCKET MAP D12
Sıraselviler Cad 63 Ⓦ tekyon.club.

Down canyon-like Sıraselviler Caddesi and best approached from the southeast corner of Taksim Square, this popular "mainstream" gay venue has a large dancefloor, a big garden out back and regular drag-shows – inevitably, it gets packed solid on Friday and Saturday evenings.

Beşiktaş and Ortaköy

The waterfront Dolmabahçe Palace, a grandiose European-style residence for the Ottoman Empire's last sultans, is the major tourist attraction this side of the Golden Horn. Northeast along the Bosphorus-front is Beşiktaş. Home to the most working class of the city's "big three" football teams, it's rapidly emerging from a cocoon of urban decay and possesses a youthful vibrancy thanks to its huge student population. Further along is Yıldız Park, a vast, wooded park dotted with imperial pavilions. Beyond it, Ortaköy retains some feel of the fishing village it once was. It has a lovely Baroque-style mosque and a lively waterfront lined with posh cafés. Just to the northeast, virtually underneath the continent-spanning Bosphorus Bridge, a handful of glitzy Bosphorus-front clubs play host to the city's glamorous elite and visiting celebrities.

Dolmabahçe Palace (Dolmabahçe Sarayı)

MAP P.114
Dolmabahçe Cad ⊕ 1 Kabataş, buses #25/E, #28 ⓦ bit.ly/DolmabahceIstanbul. Charge.

The apogee of imperial excess and home to the last sultans of the ailing Ottoman Empire after the imperial retinue moved here from Topkapı in 1853, the palace was completed in 1856. Its decidedly European appearance, influenced by the Baroque, Neoclassical and Rococo styles, makes it more akin to Versailles than a traditional Muslim palace – although it was divided, according to Islamic precepts, into an area for men only (*selamlık*) and women only (*harem*) as well as administrative quarters. Taking up a whopping 600m of Bosphorus waterfront, the palace's ornate, marble frontage is arguably best viewed from a Bosphorus cruise (see page 126). This grandiose building was primarily the work of two leading Armenian Istanbul architects, Karabet Balian and his son Nikoğos, though the showy interior, gilded with some fourteen tonnes of gold leaf, was masterminded by French decorator Sechan. The palace can only be visited as part of a guided tour, meaning visitors, usually in maximum groups of fifty, are herded through at a brisk pace. Of most interest are the hamam, complete with an incongruously luxurious squat toilet, the marquetry-work masterpiece that is the dining hall parquet floor and, in the ceremonial hall, suspended from a ceiling double the height of the other rooms, a magnificently over the top Bohemian crystal chandelier weighing 4.5 tonnes and glowing with 750 lamps, a suitably flamboyant gift from Queen Victoria.

Palace Collections Museum (Saray Koleksiyonları Müzesi)

MAP P.114
Dolmabahçe Cad ⊕ 1 Kabataş, buses #25/E, #28 ⊕ 0212 236 9000. Charge.

If you've balked at the steep admission price to the palace, it's worth checking out this unusual museum, which will give you a fascinating and more down-to-earth insight into how the opulent residence functioned. For here, displayed in what were the former kitchens of Dolmabahçe, are items in use all over the palace. They range from those you might expect, like Limoges porcelain tea services and the mother-of-pearl-inlaid wooden clogs used in the hamam, through to Singer sewing machines and, dating from the period when Atatürk was resident here, a 1930s Ericcson switchboard so crucial in a labyrinthine complex of over four hundred rooms. The kitchens themselves have been nicely restored too – needless to say, there's no gilt in sight here.

Naval Museum (Deniz Müzesi)

MAP P.114
Barbaros Meydanı ⓣ 1 Kabataş, buses #25/E, #28, #40, #40/T, #42/T

Guard at Dolmabahçe Sarayı

Ⓦ **denizmuzeleri.dzkk.tsk.tr. Charge.**
Housed in a state-of-the-art new building completed in 2013, this fine museum, with huge windows overlooking the Bosphorus, has over 20,000m of exhibition space. At the heart of the museum is a superb collection of restored caïques, elegant boats once used to row the sultans to and from their homes along the Bosphorus. The largest of these caïques, dating from 1648, needed some 144 oarsmen to propel it. Downstairs is an exhibition devoted to woodcarving in the Ottoman navy, featuring some beautiful figureheads. There's also a café and kids' play area.

Çırağan Palace (Çırağan Sarayı)

MAP P.114
Çırağan Cad ⓣ 1 Kabataş, buses #25/E, #28, #40, #40/T, #42/T.
Today the luxurious *Çırağan Palace Kempinski* (see page

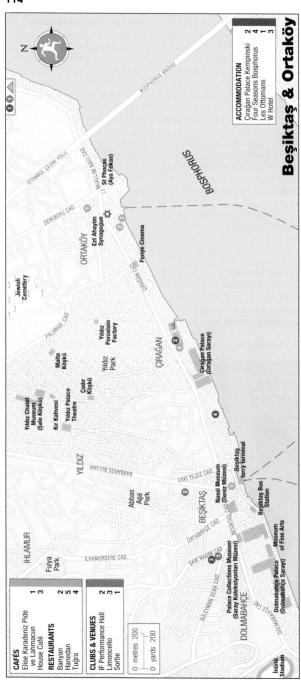

Beşiktaş & Ortaköy

ACCOMMODATION

Çirağan Palace Kempinski	2
Four Seasons Bosphorus	4
Les Ottomans	1
W Hotel	3

CAFÉS

Elise Karadeniz Pide ve Lahmacun	1
House Café	3

RESTAURANTS

Banyan	2
Hanedan	5
Tuğra	4

CLUBS & VENUES

IF Performance Hall	2
Limoncello	3
Sortie	1

0 metres 200
0 yards 200

139), this imperial residence was originally constructed in 1855 for Sultan Abdülmecit, and is very much a mini-Dolmabahçe. What you see now, however, is much more recent, as the place burned down in 1910 and was derelict until its 1990 restoration and conversion to a hotel.

Yıldız Park

MAP P.114
Cırağan Cad ● 1 Kabataş, buses #25/E, #28, #40, #40/T, #42/T.

Sprawling down a steep hillside to busy Çırağan Caddesi and the Bosphorus beyond, this oasis of green, usually entered from the south gates opposite the Çırağan Palace, was the palace complex of Abdülhamit II for thirty years. The notoriously paranoid sultan moved here from the Dolmabahçe Palace as he feared the latter was too exposed to naval attacks. Today, it's a place to escape the city hustle and/or visit the pavilions of the palace, which were designed by the famous Italian architect D'Aronco. The main points of interest are located a ten- to fifteen-minute walk uphill from the park entrance on Çırağan Caddesi. The most visited is the **Yıldız Chalet Museum** (Şale Köşkü; charge), an attractive, Swiss chalet-style pavilion dominated by the ceremonial hall which contains a 400m-square Hereke silk carpet. Here, Sultan Abdülhamit entertained Kaiser Wilhelm II in 1889 and 1898 and discussed matters of state. The **Yıldız Porcelain Factory** (charge), downhill to the southeast of the Şale Pavilion, was established in 1890 to produce china for the palace and still churns out quantities of typically florid, nineteenth-century European-style pottery which is sold in the museum shop, should such wares appeal. There are a couple of decent cafés in the grounds, one housed in another of the palace's pavilions, the pretty **Malta Köşkü**. Also worth seeking out is the **Çadır Köşkü**, another charming pavilion downhill from the Malta Köşkü, beyond the small artificial lake.

Ortaköy

MAP P.114
Buses #22, #22/RE, #25/E from Kabataş, #40, #40/T, #42/T from Taksim.

Despite being dominated by the towering Bosphorus suspension bridge, built in 1973, and surrounded by urban sprawl, Ortaköy has not entirely lost its former fishing village charm. The waterfront area, the so-called boardwalk, is today all cool cafés frequented by well-heeled Istanbulites, who come to see and be seen – and perhaps browse the artsy-craftsy Sunday morning market. The waterfront mosque, the Büyük Mecidiye Camii, is a Baroque gem built in 1854, while in the streets behind are reminders of the village's cosmopolitan past, the (invariably locked) **Ezt Ahayim synagogue** and the attractive, nineteenth-century Greek Orthodox **church of Aya Fokas** (St Phocas), the door to the walled compound of which is occasionally open.

Baked potatoes in Ortaköy

Popular with hip, young clubbers by night and families by day (especially on Sundays), Ortaköy has a ready-made market for its traditional culinary quirk – baked potatoes. Numerous stalls line the waterfront and side-streets selling red-hot varieties stuffed with virtually everything imaginable, from pungent Turkish cheeses and olives to spicy sausages and tuna.

Cafés

Elise Karadeniz Pide ve Lahmacun

MAP P.114
Eski Bahçe Sok 4, Beşiktaş.
Ⓦ elisepidelahmacun.com.
Long-established and bustling *pide*
(Turkish pizza) place run by Black
Sea emigres, they cook a wide-
variety of succulent *pide* in their
wood-fired oven, as well as two
types of *lahmacun* and the shredded
wheat, honey and cheese dessert,
künefe. €

House Café

MAP P.114
Salhane Sok 1. Buses #25/E, #28, #40,
#40/T, #42 Ⓦ thehousecafe.com.
A stylish, upmarket café whose
concept has proven so popular
there are now nine spread across the
city. This has to be the best located,
with views over the waterfront and
Ortaköy's Baroque-style mosque,
and it is housed in a lovingly
converted turn-of-the-nineteenth-
century building. Posh pastas,
burgers and the like are the staple,
Sunday brunch a metropolitan's
favourite. Licensed. €€

Restaurants

Banyan

MAP P.114
Salhane Sok 3. Buses #25/E, #28, #40,
#40/T, #42 Ⓦ banyanrestaurant.com.
Like its near neighbour and
rival the *House Café*, this place
concentrates on giving its loyal,
largely youthful local clientele
something a bit different, with
Asian-fusion cuisine taking centre
stage – from Indian to Vietnamese.
It's not cheap, but it's decent
quality and the views of the
Bosphorus Bridge and boardwalk
are great. Licensed. €€€

Hanedan

MAP P.114
Ciğdem Sok 27. Buses #25/E, #2,8 #40,

Banyan

#40/T, #42 ⓦ hanedanrestorant.com.
Established in 1983, this
restaurant has a lively location
next to Beşiktaş pier. The
downstairs is given over to grilled
meat dishes, the upstairs to
seafood. There's a great selection
of meze and a wide choice of fish,
both farmed and wild caught. It's
not as swish as some Bosphorus-
front places and consequently
better value, with fish sold by
weight. Licensed. €€€

Tuğra

MAP P.114
Çırağan Palace Kempinski Hotel, Çırağan
Cad 32. Buses #25/E, #40, #40/T, #42
ⓦ kempinski.com.
Appropriately expensive place
located in this former palace, but
worth it for the lovely Bosphorus
views from the candle-lit terrace,
attentive service and quality
Ottoman-style dishes. Also in the
hotel is the *Laledan* restaurant,
noted for monumental breakfasts
(300-plus items), Sunday brunches
and seafood evening meals.
Licensed. €€€€

Clubs & venues

IF Performance Hall

MAP P.114
Hasfirin Cad 26. ⓦ ifperformance.com.
One of the best live music venues
with architecture perfect for large
concerts, being spacious and
offering clear views of the stage
from every point. The staff are very
friendly, polite and caring. You
can buy tickets either at the door
or through ⓦ biletix.com, though
make sure to check beforehand
which of the two applies for a
specific event. There are sometimes
some sound issues in the smoking
section.

Limoncello

MAP P.114
Süleyman Seba Cad 34.
ⓦ eksenistanbul.com.

Tuğra

An urban, colourful and modern
club with an intriguing ambiance.
Plays a mix of Turkish and
Western music. The attractive
garden is the place to go to talk,
as the sound of the music is kept
low. They have excellent cocktails
with fresh fruit and some decent
international cuisine as well as
great desserts.

Sortie

MAP P.114
Muallım Naci Cad 141/2. Buses #25/E, #28,
#40, #40/T, #42 ⓦ sortie.com.tr.
This sophisticated Bosphorus-
front place plays a mix of house
and pop, and though it has pretty
steep admission fees at weekends
(free through the week) you do
get a drink on the house. As
it's spread across 3500 square
metres, there's plenty of room
for Istanbul's fashionable elite
to see and, more importantly,
be seen. *Sortie* also attracts
wealthy party animals from the
Middle East and beyond. A
series of nine themed restaurants
– Mediterranean, sushi, South
American, fish etc – are all part of
the concept.

Asian Istanbul

Worth it for the bargain-priced ferry-ride from Europe to Asia alone, a few hours spent exploring conservative Üsküdar or bustling Kadıköy will enhance your Istanbul experience. The former of these suburbs, known to nineteenth-century visitors such as Florence Nightingale as Scutari, has several impressive Ottoman mosques within easy walking distance of the ferry terminal or Üsküdar Marmaray line metro stop as well as the Maiden's Tower, an offshore lighthouse that figured in Bond thriller *The World is Not Enough*. Kadıköy has transformed itself into a mini-Beyoğlu over the last few years and is great for shopping, eating and nightlife. It's also home to the pretty 1920s Süreyya Opera House and one of the city's best restaurants, *Çiya Sofrası*. Adjoining Kadıköy to the north is Haydarpaşa, with its imposing, early twentieth-century railway station, Florence Nightingale Museum and British Crimean War Cemetery.

Üsküdar and its Ottoman Mosques

MAP P.120, POCKET MAP N4
Regular ferries from Eminönü and Karaköy: Daily 6.40am–11pm; last ferry back 10.30pm. Charge. Marmaray line metro trains run under the Bosphorus from Sirkeci.

Üsküdar ferry terminal is more or less opposite the **Mihrimah Camii**, built in 1547–1548. Like its namesake out by the city's land walls (see page 79), this fine mosque was designed for the favourite daughter of Süleyman the Magnificent, Mihrimah, by the skilled and prolific architect Sinan (see page 59). It was built on a raised terrace and is curious in design terms because, rather than using the conventional central dome flanked by two or four semi-domes, the Mihrimah Camii has three semi-domes. Around 500m to the southwest, on the far side of the Üsküdar stop of the trans-Bosphorus Marmaray metro line (see page 147), is the very

attractive **Şemsi Paşa Camii**. Built in 1580, again a work of Sinan, it is set right on the water's edge. The tomb of the grand vizier for whom it was constructed, Şemsi Paşa, is located in the grounds. A little over half a kilometre inland, the **Yeni Valide Camii**, built at the behest of Ahmet III for his mother, was completed in 1710. Its most distinguished feature is the valide sultan's tomb, encased in an aviary-like mesh. Further inland is the **Atik Valide Külliyesi**, a mosque complex once again attributable to the ubiquitous Sinan, dating to 1583. Its courtyard is attractive and there's a small, traditional teahouse where you can sip sweet black tea with mosque-going regulars. Further east is the **Çinili Camii** and its associated hamam. Dating to 1640, the mosque is generally locked, but look helpless and the caretaker should appear to let you into the prayer hall. The historic **Çinili Hamamı** is just below the mosque (Çavuşdere Cad

Getting around by ferry

Üsküdar's major sights are all within easy walking distance of the ferry terminal and Marmaray metro stop. Everything worth seeing or doing in Kadıköy lies just a short walk from the ferry terminal. But if you come for an evening meal or drink, double-check the times of the last ferry or metro back. Note that you can reach Kadıköy from Üsküdar by taking the Marmaray metro one stop to Ayrılık Çeşmesi then changing to the M4 metro for Kadıköy.

204, ⓦcinilihamam.com). The building dates back to 1684, is clean without being antiseptic and the prices are a fraction of those in the old city's tourist-orientated bathhouses – but don't expect any English to be spoken.

The Maiden's Tower (Kız Kulesi)

MAP P.120, POCKET MAP M4
Salacak. Charge for museum.
A little over a kilometre south of the Üsküdar ferry terminal is a small pier where boats take visitors to the landmark tower (ⓦkizkulesi.gov.tr, entry fee includes return boat ride). Also known as Leander's Tower, it was built in the fifth century BC to control ships using the Bosphorus.

The Byzantines stretched a chain between it and another tower at the tip of the peninsula to block enemy ships and in the Ottoman era it became a lighthouse. The iconic tower underwent major restoration in 2022 and the views from the tower, up and down the Bosphorus and back across to the old city, are great.

Kadıköy

MAP P.122
Regular ferries from Eminönü: Daily 7.20am–9.10pm, last ferry back 8.30pm; from Karaköy 6.35am to midnight, last ferry back 1am. Charge.
The heart of this lively suburb is south of the heaving waterfront, in the narrow grid of streets beyond Söğütlüçeşme Caddesi. In the late

Şemsi Ahmet Paşa Camii

Üsküdar

RESTAURANT
Kanaat Lokantası — 1

Çinili Camii
Çinili Hamamı
Bülbüldere Cemetery
Atik Valide Külliyesi
Mihrimah Camii
HAKİMİYETİ
ÜSKÜDAR
Yeni Valide Camii
Üsküdar ferry terminal
Şemsi Paşa Camii
ÜSKÜDAR HAREM SAHİL YOLU
Salacak ferry terminal
The Maiden's Tower (Kız Kulesi)
SEA OF MARMARA
N
0 metres 200
0 yards 200

Kız Kulesi

nineteenth and early twentieth centuries this area was home to a well to do, predominantly Greek, Armenian, and foreign population, a prosperity which is reflected in the domestic architecture of fine European-style town houses and stylish shop fronts. Look out for these older buildings among the more recent concrete ones, notably the cream curves of the Art Deco *Kurukhaveci Mehmet Efendi* coffee outlet. Pedestrianized **Güneşlibahçe Sokak** is well known for its permanent street market, quality delis and fruit, vegetable and fish stalls. Nearby are a couple of architecturally undistinguished but interesting churches, the Greek Orthodox Aya Eufemia and the Armenian church of Surp Takvor. Both are likely to be closed except for Sunday morning services. The area bounded by Söğütlüçeşme Caddesi to the north, Bahariye and Emin Bay *caddesi*s to the east and south and the Bosphorus waterfront to the west is a vibrant area of alternative clothing outlets, antique and bric-a-brac shops, cafes, bars and restaurants all

spilling out onto the busy, narrow streets. The pick of the numerous restaurants here is *Çiya Sofrası* (see page 124). Further inland is the beautiful **Süreyya Opera House** (Bahariye Cad 29 ☎ 0216 346 1531), a 1920s gem with a Neoclassical façade of relief-work cherubs and Classical-style theatre masks. Its regular winter programme of opera, ballet and classical music is popular with the largely secular-minded Istanbulites who favour Kadıköy over more conservative parts of the city. A little further east is the Rüştü Saraçoğlu stadium, home to Turkey's richest club, **Fenerbahçe**. Nearby Bağdat (Baghdad) Caddesi offers more mainstream, upmarket shopping opportunities than those found around **Güneşlibahçe Sokak**, and is where well-heeled youngsters come to show off their fancy cars and expensive clothes.

Toy Museum (Oyuncak Müzesi)

MAP P.122
Dr Zeki Zeren Sok, Göztepe. Buses #GZ1, #GZ2, #10, #10/B from Kadıköy. ⓦ istanbuloyuncakmuzesi.com. Charge.

Kadıköy

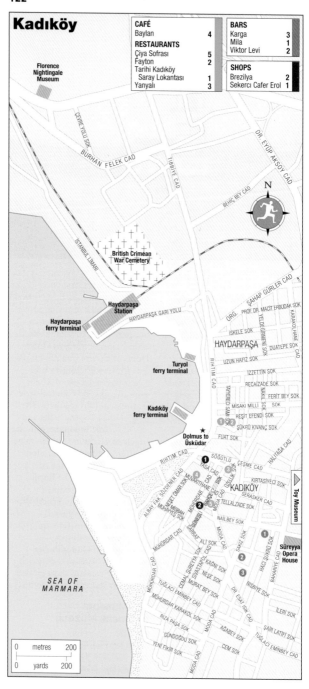

Florence Nightingale Museum

ÇEVRE YOLU SOK

BURHAN FELEK CAD

TIBBIYE CAD

BEHIÇ BEY CAD

DR. EYÜP AKSOY CAD

N

İSTANBUL LİMANI

British Crimean War Cemetery

Haydarpaşa Station

Haydarpaşa ferry terminal

HAYDARPAŞA GARI YOLU

ORG. ŞAHAP GÜRLER CAD

ORG. PROF. DR. MACIT ERBUDAK SOK

YELDEĞİRMENİ SOK

KARAKOLHANE CAD

İSKELE SOK

DUATEPE SOK

HAYDARPAŞA

RIHTIM CAD

UZUN HAFIZ SOK

Turyol ferry terminal

TAYYERED CAM SOK

İZZETTİN SOK

RECAIZADE SOK

NAKIL SOK

FERIT BEY SOK

MİSAKİ MİLLİ SOK

REŞIT EFENDI SOK

ŞÜKRÜ KIVANÇ SOK

Kadıköy ferry terminal

★ **Dolmuş to Üsküdar**

FUAT SOK

RIHTIM CAD

SÖĞÜTLÜ

YASA CAD

ÇEŞME CAD

HALİTAĞA CAD

ALBAY FAIK SÖZDENER CAD

MÜHÜRDAR HANE CAD

NEŞET ÖMER SOK

MİSBAH MUHAYYEŞ SOK

MÜHÜRDAR CAD

MODA CAD

SERASKER CAD

KIRTASİYECİ SOK

KADIKÖY

TELLALZADE SOK

NAİLBEY SOK

SARRAF ALI SOK

SAKIZ SOK

HACI ŞÜKRÜ SOK

BAHARİYE CAD

Süreyya Opera House

MÜHÜRDAR CAD

CEMAL SÜREYYA CAD

SIVASTAPOL CAD

KADNI SOK

NEŞE SOK

MURAT BEY SOK

DR. ESAT IŞIK CAD

NİSBİYE SOK

MODA CAD

İLERİ SOK

SEA OF MARMARA

TUĞLACI EMİNBEY CAD

MÜHÜRDAR KARAKOL CAD

RIZA PAŞA SOK

GÜNDOĞDU SOK

YENI FIKIR SOK

MODA CAD

AĞABEY SOK

CEM SOK

ŞAİR LATİFİ SOK

TUĞLACI EMİNBEY CAD

▷ Toy Museum

| 0 | metres | 200 |
| 0 | yards | 200 |

Appropriately housed in what was, until the 1950s, one of the city's best toyshops, this museum has a fine collection of toys drawn mainly from Western Europe and North America. Many exhibits are displayed in themed rooms, and there is everything here from teddy bears to Barbies, though best are the tin toys.

Haydarpaşa Station

MAP P.122
A handful of ferries from Karaköy call here – consult the timetables.

Haydarpaşa station is well remembered by millions of Turks who arrived in the big city from villages and towns across Anatolia in the big waves of rural–urban migration between the 1950s and 1990s. German Gothic in style, it was built in 1908 as part of the ambitious Berlin-to-Baghdad railway, a gift from Kaiser Wilhelm II to Sultan Abdülhamit II, and is built on 1100 piles sunk into the Bosphorus. The station has been bypassed by the Marmaray metro project and was badly damaged by a fire in 2010, with restoration work set to be completed in 2024.

Obelisk, British Crimean War Cemetery

British Crimean War Cemetery

MAP P.122
TİBBİYE /Burhan Felek Cad, GATA yanı. Buses #12, #1/A from Kadıköy.

Attractively laid out beneath elegantly tapering cypress and spreading plane trees are the graves and tombs of some 6000 British soldiers who lost their lives in the Crimean War (1853–56). Most were victims of cholera which swept through the nearby military hospital in Scutari (today's Selimiye) barracks established by Florence Nightingale rather than battleground casualties. As well as victims of the Crimean War, there are over 700 civilians, and 450 Commonwealth soldiers from both world wars. The single most obvious monument is an obelisk decorated with four angels holding wreaths at each corner, erected at the behest of Queen Victoria in 1857. The cemetery, beautifully maintained by the Commonwealth War Graves Commission, is tricky to find on your own – it may be best to get a taxi in Kadıköy or Haydarpaşa. The entrance is by the *Acıl* (emergency) department of the GATA military hospital (*GATA Asker Hastanesi*).

ASIAN ISTANBUL

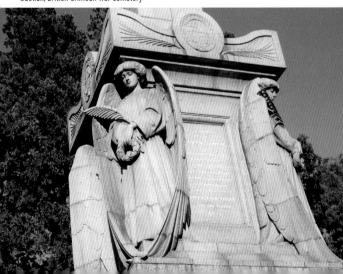

Shops

Brezilya

MAP P.122

Guneşlibahçe Sok 21, Kadıköy.

Much cheaper than the famed *Kurukhaveci Mehmet Efendi* coffee purveyors in Eminönü and Kadıköy, this place has been grinding coffee since 1920. It's also great for the healthy Turkish delicacy *pestil*, sheets of dried fruit molasses (usually apricot, grape, plum and mulberry) and other deli delights.

Şekercı Cafer Erol

MAP P.122

Yasa Cad 19, Kadıköy

Ⓦ sekercicafererol.com.

Even if you don't buy anything it's worth visiting this time-warp sweet shop for its wonderful window and counter displays, which accurately reflect the foundation date of this branch of the store in 1945 (though the family business has been going for over 200 years). Try the exquisitely attractive marzipan fruits, which in fact look far too precious to eat, or the more prosaic *alkide*, boiled sweets.

Şekercı Cafer Erol

Café

Baylan

MAP P.122

Muvakithane Cad 19, Kadıköy

Ⓦ baylangida.com.

A relic of a bygone era but still going strong, this patisserie has a narrow, 1950s wood-and-chrome frontage and is famous for its eye-catching mini-macaroons, each a different pastel shade. There's respite from the hurly-burly outside in the vine-shaded garden. The perfect afternoon tea stop after a shopping expedition in Asia. €

Restaurants

Çiya Sofrası

MAP P.122

Guneşlibahçe Sok 43, Kadıköy

Ⓦ ciya.com.tr.

Offering one of the most varied menus in Istanbul, this superb restaurant is actually three separate places either adjacent to or opposite each other on this pedestrianized street, and has become a major incentive to visit the Asian side of the city. Dishes on offer are drawn from all over

Turkey and adjacent Middle-Eastern countries. Most popular at lunchtimes is the outlet on the east side of the alley, where you choose from a tempting array of meze, salads and *sulu yemek* (stew-type dishes), and have your plate weighed to find out the damage. The two outlets on the other side of the street do superb kebabs. Unlicensed. €€

Fayton

MAP P.122
Tayyareci Sami Sok 2
Ⓦ faytonrestaurant.com.tr.

This place used to be a blacksmith's shop and has been beautifully resorted and converted into a small, family-run restaurant. The cuisine is a mix of Greek and Turkish, and the fixed menu, which includes a couple of drinks as well as starters, main and dessert, is good value. €€

Kanaat Lokantası

MAP P.120, POCKET MAP O3
Selmanipak Cad 25, Üsküdar Ⓣ 0216 553 3791.

Established back in 1931, this genteel *lokanta* makes a very worthwhile lunch-stop if you're exploring conservative Üsküdar's backstreets. There's a wide range of starters, both hot and cold, as well as a fantastic choice of mains and desserts – many of them quite different to those found in the average Turkish restaurant – such as Circassian chicken in walnut sauce. Unlicensed. €

Tarihi Kadıköy Saray Lokantası

MAP P.122
Yoğurtlu Şükrü Sok 7, Kadıköy Ⓣ 0216 346 2262.

Bustling old school tradesman's restaurant just off Rihtim Caddesi, dishing up everything from hearty stews to grills and a range of desserts. There are a few tables outside and it is deservedly busy – especially at lunchtimes. Unlicenced. €

Yanyalı

MAP P.122
Yağlıka İsmail Sok 1, Kadıköy Ⓣ 0216 336 3333.

Similar to Üsküdar's *Kanaat*, but even older, having been established by émigrés from Greece in 1919, it's not a place to come for trendy, fusion cuisine, or even pizza or a burger. Instead there are some twenty varieties of soup on offer, a whole range of different stews including some oven-cooked in clay dishes, and a wide range of desserts including tahini-drenched candied pumpkin (*kabak tatlisi*). Unlicensed. €

Bars

Karga

MAP P.122
Kadife Sok 16, Kadıköy Ⓣ 0216 449 1725.

Blurring the line between bar, alternative art gallery and café, this is where black-clad students and alternative-types come to drink beer, smoke (in the garden out back), chat and perhaps sample something from the bar-snack menu.

Mila

MAP P.122
Miralay Nazim Sok 6, Kadıköy Ⓦ milawinehouse.com.

This is a charming, small, rustic wine bar hidden in one of Kadıköy's side streets. There's a very pleasant little backyard that you can enjoy your meal or wine in on a warm day. If there's a crowd, there may be a little wait for your food, but the friendliness of the staff will more than make up for it.

Viktor Levi

MAP P.122
Damacı Sok 4, Kadıköy Ⓣ 0216 449 9329.

Much more mainstream than *Karga*, *Viktor Levi* is housed in a substantial, late nineteenth-century house ranged around a pleasant garden. It's been making house wines since the 1920s and they are both reasonably priced and palatable enough. Extensive menu too.

The Bosphorus and Princes' Islands

Few visitors to a city where the sea is so much a part of its being can resist the temptation of a boat trip up the Bosphorus. Over 31km long but a mere 700m wide at its narrowest point, the strait connects the Black and Marmara seas as well as separating Europe from Asia. Many of the impressive sights along the Bosphorus can be seen from the water; to explore them, the intrepid can take a bus from the city centre. The pretty Princes' Islands are just 35 minutes away by sea bus, a little longer by regular ferry. Here you can admire fin de siècle villas, ride in an electric car through pine-scented hills, hire a bike and, in summer, swim in the Sea of Marmara.

Bosphorus Cruises

The long, six-hour Bosphorus cruise run by Şehir Hatları (see page 147) is a highlight of any visit to Istanbul. Tickets can be bought from the Boğaz Ferry Terminal just east of the Galata Bridge in Eminönü, with boats departing daily at 10.35am year-round. Drinks and snacks are available on board, as the only lengthy stop is a 2.5hr layover at peaceful Anadolu Kavağı village, on the strait's Asian side. En route, brief stops are made at Beşiktaş (Europe), Kanlıca (Asia), Sariyer and Rumeli Kavağı (both Europe). You can get off at any

Bosphorus cruises, Rumeli Hisarı

Borusan Contemporary

of these points (one-way tickets are available) but you'll have to take a bus back to the city centre. Travelling north, on the European shore you'll see Dolmabahçe Palace and Ortaköy before passing under the first Bosphorus Bridge, with **Beylerbeyi Palace** (see page 127) on the Asian shore virtually under the bridge. Back on the European side you'll pass **Arnavutköy** and **Bebek**, once sleepy fishing villages turned prosperous suburbs. Before the second bridge rises, you'll see the landmark **Rumeli Hisarı** fortress (see page 128) and on the Asian side a good example of a *yalı* (Ottoman-era waterfront mansion), the **Köprülü Amcazade Hüesyin Paşa Yalı**. Beyond the second bridge is the **Sakıp Sabancı Museum** (see page 128). Try the sugared yoghurt brought on by vendors at **Kanlıca**, then on the European side look out for **Sait Halim Paşa Yalı** at Yeniköy, an Art Nouveau delight. Sariyer is home to the **Sadberk Hanım Museum** (see page 129). The strait becomes less built up

as you approach the layover point at **Anadolu Kavağı**, where most visitors are content to stretch their legs and enjoy a cheap fish meal in green, quiet surroundings, though there's a Byzantine fortress to clamber up to for the energetic.

Other cruises include Şehir Hatları's short tour from Eminönü to Ortaköy departing daily at 2.40 pm and at 3.30pm and private operator Turyol has 1.5hr-long tours up to the second (Fatih Mehmet Sultan) bridge at least hourly between 10am and 9pm, more frequently on summer weekends. Alternatively from mid-June to the end of September only there's a Şehir Hatları Saturday-night cruise (Mehtaplı) departing Eminönü at 6.25pm, which goes as far as Anadolu Kavağı.

Beylerbeyi Palace

MAP P.128
Abdullah Ağa Cad 12. Buses #15, #15/B from Üsküdar ☏ 0216 321 9320. Charge.
An even grander take on the grand *yalı*s (waterfront mansions) lining the Bosphorus, this nineteenth-century marble pile was the

summer residence and guesthouse of late Ottoman sultans. Entrance is expensive, but if European-style palace architecture is your thing it may appeal – and it has attractive gardens.

Borusan Contemporary

MAP P.128
Perili Köşk, 5 Hisar Cad. Buses #40, and #40/T from Taksim, #22, #22/RE and #25/E from Kabataş ⓦ borusancontemporary.com. Charge.
This unique contemporary arts centre operates as the headquarters of Borusan Holdings during the week, but is open on Saturday and Sunday for art lovers, with all kinds of installations, sculptures and photographs. The building itself, in the shadow of the second Bosphorus Bridge, is a striking ten-storey brick-built mansion begun in 1910, which soon became known as the Perili Köşk ("Haunted Mansion").

Rumeli Hisarı

MAP P.128
Yahya Kemal Cad 42. Buses #22, #25/E, #40, #40/T ⓣ 0212 263 5305. Charge.
Superb fortification of six towers joined by curtain walling just before the second suspension bridge (Fatih Sultan Mehmet), Rumeli Hisarı was built in 1452 as part of Sultan Mehmet's plans to capture Constantinople. Working in tandem with the **Anadolu Hisarı** fort, still visible across the strait in Asia, it effectively blocked the Bosphorus to enemy ships and cut off aid to the beleaguered Byzantines.

Sakıp Sabancı Museum

MAP P.128
Sakıp Sabancı Cad. Buses #22, #25/E, #40, #40/T ⓦ sakipsabancimuzesi.org. Charge.
Housed in a beautifully restored 1920s waterfront villa, this superb museum-cum-gallery hosts major exhibitions, which in the past have included the likes of Dalí

The Bosphorus

Sakıp Sabancı Museum

and Picasso. In addition, there's a good permanent collection of Ottoman-era calligraphy and works by nineteenth- and twentieth-century Turkish artists. Just up the waterfront is **Emirgan Parkı**, the city's most attractive park, with some lovely turn-of-the-century pavilions and fine stands of tulips in April.

Sadberk Hanım Museum

MAP P.128
Büyükdere Cad 27–29. Buses #25/E, #40, #40/T ⓦ sadberkhanimmuzesi.org.tr. Charge.

This pair of turn-of-the-nineteenth-century waterfront houses has been lovingly converted into a satisfying museum. The house on the right as you enter is given over to mainly Ottoman-period artefacts, including some fine ceramics, as well as rooms mocked-up as they would have been in the nineteenth century. The house on the left is home to a private collection of small but top-quality artefacts collected from Anatolia, from Urartian bronze work to Attic red-figure vases to Hellenistic gold jewellery to Roman figurines.

Kınalıada

MAP P.130
Ferries and sea buses dock at the island's sole settlement on the east coast, where there are plenty of cafés and restaurants. There's little to see on this rather barren outcrop, bar the church of **Surp Krikor Lusavoriç**, up the hill behind the waterfront. Built in 1857, it is notable for its windows, painted nostalgically with famous churches from the Armenians' homeland in what is now Eastern Turkey. The Istanbul Armenians, who make up most of the island's (mainly summer-only) community, keep this symbol of their faith in immaculate condition. The island takes its Turkish name Kınalıada or "Henna Island" from its red cliffs. You can bike around the island too.

Burgazada

MAP P.130
Again, essentially a single settlement clustering around the ferry terminal, Burgazada is green and partially forested. The little town is dotted with some nice wooden villas, mostly shrouded by oleander, fig and palm trees, and

is home to the large, nineteenth-century Greek Orthodox **Church of St John the Baptist**. Also in the backstreets you'll find the **Sait Faik Museum** on Burgaz Çayırı Sok 15 (☎0216 381 2060, free). The house of Sait Faik, a bohemian whose short stories chronicled the harsh lives of the poor, has been well preserved – down to the pyjamas folded on his bed. If you're feeling energetic, hire a bike and explore – one worthwhile stop is **Kalpazankaya**, where you can swim and eat in a decent restaurant of the same name. Alternatively, ride here in an electric car as part of an island tour. There's decent accommodation at *Mehtap 45* (see page 140).

Heybeliada

MAP P.130

Larger and more popular as a day or weekend outing than either Kınalıada or Burgazada,

this attractive island gets its name, Heybeliada or "**Island of the Saddlebag**", from the twin hills that dominate it. The small settlement where the ferry docks, on the east coast, has numerous pretty fin de siècle villas, including one where the family of novelist Orhan Pamuk (see page 100) summered. Again, there are plenty of places to eat and drink in town and a limited choice of places to stay (see page 139).

In town is an imposing **Naval School** (Deniz Harp Okulu) and the Greek Orthodox **Church of Aya Nikola**, curiously adorned with a clock tower. Like all the islands, it's traffic-free so the best way to get around is by phaeton, a horse-drawn carriage (tours start from Ayyıldız Caddesi behind the waterfront), though a bicycle hired from one of several outlets near the jetty works out much cheaper and gives more flexibility. Best of

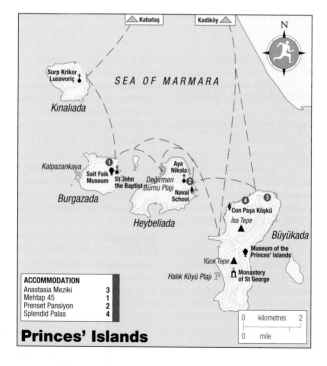

ACCOMMODATION

Anastasia Meziki	3
Mehtap 45	1
Prenset Pansiyon	2
Splendid Palas	4

Princes' Islands

Getting to the Princes' Islands

In Byzantine times home to monasteries and banished royalty, and at the turn of the nineteenth century to the city's wealthy Christian minorities, the islands today (Adalar in Turkish) are a popular escape. The jump-off point is Kabataş, from where **Şehir Hatları** ferries run up to the four main islands using the İstanbulkart travel card (see page 144). The ferries stop at Kadıköy on the Asian shore before continuing to the islands. Several companies operate smaller boats for a slightly higher price. All of these boats take around an hour and a half to reach Büyükada, the biggest island, and fifty minutes to the smallest and nearest, Kınalıada. Turyol boats run from Karaköy, Denturavrasya from Beşiktaş.

the three beach clubs is **Değirmen Burnu Plajı** (charge) on the northwest coast, a shingle strip at the foot of cliffs in a pine forest.

Büyükada

MAP P.130

This is by far the most visited of the Princes' Islands. The visitors milling around the ferry terminal of the main settlement can be off-putting, but hire a bike or walk and you're soon away from the crowds. The most sumptuous of the islands' wooden mansions, once owned by wealthy Jewish and Greek families, are on Büyükada, many on the shore west of the Art Nouveau **Splendid Palas** hotel (see page 140). One roofless and abandoned house below the splendid wooden mansion **Con Paşa Köşkü**, on Çankaya Caddesi, was home to **Trotsky**, who started the *History of the Russian Revolution* while exiled here between 1929 and 1933. Again, you can explore by phaeton or bicycle (try Trek on Nisan Cad 23, near the clock tower), with a round island trip taking about an hour and a half. There's plenty to see, not least the **Monastery of St George** (usually open; free) on **Yüce Tepe**, a prominent pine-covered hill. It's about a fifteen-minute walk to the summit and bikes are not allowed. On the east of the island the **Museum of the Princes' Islands** (adalarmuzesi.

org, charge) has an exhibition about the island's writers and poets and nearby is the charming boutique *Ayanikola Butik* hotel. There are several places to swim; by far the most peaceful is the **Halik Köyü Plajı** (charge), reached by steep steps from the road running around the island some 3km south of the town. Many views from the islands inevitably at least partially include the urban sprawl of the metropolis, but here you have lovely views across the Sea of Marmara to its distant, wooded south shore.

Phaeton

ACCOMMODATION

Pool at the Four Seasons Bosphorus

Accommodation

Most visitors choose to stay around Sultanahmet, the heart of the old city, where there is a high concentration of hotels, pensions and hostels, as well as the major sights. Inevitably given the demand, many establishments have opened on the fringes of Sultanahmet – in Sirkeci and towards the Grand Bazaar. Ever more visitors, particularly those for whom nightlife and contemporary arts and culture are as important as historical sights, are basing themselves across the Golden Horn in trendy Galata and Beyoğlu. If you're looking for exclusivity, a pricey Bosphorus-front hotel may well appeal, while those looking to spend a night on an island retreat may be tempted by the Princes' Islands. Kadıköy, on the Asian side of the city, has become the district of choice for many younger, secular-orientated Istanbulites, and its many bars and low-key eating places have made it popular with visitors of a similar profile, too.

Sultanahmet

AGORA GUEST HOUSE & HOSTEL MAP P.26, POCKET MAP H12. Amiral Tafdil Sok 6 ⓘ 1 Sultanahmet ⓦ agoraguesthouse. com. A hip and successful cross between a guesthouse and hostel in a quiet street off busy Akbıyık Caddesi, one of its best points is the stylish communal lounge fronted by a terrace. There are ten en-suite double rooms and dorms ranging from four- to ten-beds – including one female-only. The one downside is the small number of shared bathrooms. Dorms €, doubles €€

ALP MAP P.26, POCKET MAP J12. Akbıyık Cad, Adliye Sok 4 ⓘ 1 Sultanahmet ⓦ alpguesthouse.com. Period-style hotel down a quiet alley off bustling, tourist-central Akbıyık Caddesi. The rooms are on the small side but tastefully done-out with

Getting a room

All prices are for the cheapest double room in high season, which for most establishments is mid-March to mid-November and Christmas/New Year – though many places have reductions in July and August. Low-season rates are usually fifteen to twenty percent less. Don't be afraid to ask for a reduction – bargaining is part of the culture – and some smaller places will offer a discount (between five and ten percent) for payment in cash.

Breakfast is included in all places listed except apartments; the vast majority have air conditioning to cope with the city's sultry summers, and double glazing and central heating for the sometimes cold, damp winters. Free Wi-fi is also a given in all but the more expensive chain hotels. Istanbul is an international city, and the vast majority of hotels quote their prices in euros to reflect their clientele.

Accommodation price codes

Pricing (in €) is based on a standard double room for one night in peak season not including breakfast (unless otherwise stated)

€ = €20–70
€€ = €70–120
€€€ = €120–250
€€€€ = over €250

wood floors, rugs, pale walls with dark-wood trim – and some have four-poster beds. The partly enclosed roof terrace has good views of the entrance to the Bosphorus, as do a few of the rooms. €€

CHEERS MAP P.26, POCKET MAP H10. Zeynepsultan Camii Sok 21 ① 1 Sultanahmet ⓦ cheershostel. com. More subtle than its Sultanahmet rivals, this hostel is nicely located on a quiet side street in a characterful early twentieth-century house. It has a range of well-kitted-out rooms, from doubles to four- and ten-bed dorms. One major plus is the upstairs bar, with a terrace affording a picture-postcard view of the Haghia Sophia. Friendly and well managed too. **Dorms/doubles €**

CHEERS LIGHTHOUSE MAP P.26, POCKET MAP G9. Çayıroğlu Sok 18 ① 1 Sultanahmet ⓦ cheershostel.com. Part of a new wave of hostel accommodation in the city, it provides hotel-like facilities without losing the communal hostel feel. The five rooms here range from a six-bed dorm to a luxury penthouse, with some facing a quiet street, others the sea, a stone's throw away across the defunct suburban railway line. There's free coffee and an excellent in-house restaurant. **Dorms/doubles €**

DENİZ HOUSES MAP P.26, POCKET MAP G9. Çayıroğlu Sok 14 ① 1 Sultanahmet ⓦ denizhouses.com. Two adjoining period buildings, down a quiet alley below the major concentration of hotels on and around Akbıyık Caddesi, make up this well-run establishment. Rooms in A block are small but homely, with stripped wood floors and Turkish rugs. Front rooms have sea views (for a higher price) but get some noise from the suburban railway below.

B Block rooms are larger and quieter but there are no sea views – go up to the pleasant roof terrace for these. €

EMPRESS ZOE MAP P.26, POCKET MAP J12. Akbıyık Cad, Adliye Sok 10 ① 1 Sultanahmet ⓦ emzoe.com. You can't get much more historic than a hotel built over the remains of an Ottoman bathhouse, which itself stands on the basement wall of a Byzantine palace. The American owners have stamped their distinctive mark on this treasure of a boutique hotel which, despite the rather small rooms and tricky layout, makes for a wonderfully atmospheric stay in the heart of the old city. Book direct for a 10% discount. €€

FOUR SEASONS SULTANAHMET MAP P.26, POCKET MAP H12. Tevfikhane Sok 1 ① 1 Sultanahmet ⓦ fourseasons. com For anyone with a desire to spend a night in a former prison (*not* the one Billy Hayes was incarcerated in *Midnight Express*), this luxury hotel may fit in the bill. The rooms are palatial, with all the mod-cons you'd expect. The Neoclassical architecture is splendid, the situation excellent – it backs, controversially, onto Byzantine substructures being turned into an "archeology park" – and you don't have to slop out. Underwent a major upgrade/renovation in 2023. €€€€

HANEDAN MAP P.26, POCKET MAP J12. Akbıyık Cad, Adliye Sok 3 ① 1 Sultanahmet ⓦ hanedanhotel.com. This is one of the best affordable hotels in Cankurtaran, run by a knowledgeable partnership of four friends. The standard rooms have king-sized beds sitting on dark wooden boards, pastel-coloured walls and dark wood furniture. The triple and family rooms have four-poster beds and there are good views from the roof terrace. €

IBRAHIM PAŞA MAP P.26, POCKET MAP G12. Terzihane Sok 5 🚇 1 Sultanahmet ⓦ ibrahimpasha.com. Superb blend of old and new in this lovingly converted pair of nineteenth-century townhouses, quietly located just off the Hippodrome. Bare boards, tasteful rugs and a successful blend of antique furniture and contemporary fittings are the basics of the mix of standard and deluxe rooms. Fabulous roof terrace with sweeping sea and old city views, a charming lounge with open fire downstairs and friendly, professional staff. €€€

KYBELE MAP P.26, POCKET MAP G11. Yerebatan Cad 35 🚇 1 Sultanahmet ⓦ kybelehotel.com. Characterful boutique hotel run by three outgoing brothers, the *Kybele* has been fashioned from a distinctive rendered-brick terraced house. Forget it if minimalism is your thing, because this place is crammed with vintage artefacts and has over 4000 antique/period-style light fittings. The sixteen rooms have brass beds and stripped wood floors, while out back is a quiet garden and reading area. €€

NOMADE MAP P.26, POCKET MAP G11. Ticarethane Sok 15 🚇 1 Sultanahmet ⓦ hotelnomade.com.tr. One of the old city's earliest designer boutique hotels, the *Nomade* retains its family atmosphere and attention to detail. Rooms are on the small side and breakfast might run a little late, but it represents good value for money in what has become an over-priced part of the city. Great roof-terrace bar too, with superb views of the Haghia Sophia. €€

OTTOMAN HOTEL IMPERIAL MAP P.26, POCKET MAP H11. Caferiye Sok 6/1 🚇 1 Sultanahmet ⓦ ottomanhotelimperial. com. A well-run period-style hotel right in the heart of Sultanahmet, offering a wide range of plush rooms conservatively kitted-out with dark wood furniture and shiny bedspreads. The views from the premium rooms especially are stunning, with the magnificent Haghia Sophia dominating the scene. Attached is the *Matbah* restaurant (see page 40), well known for its Ottoman cuisine. €€

PENINSULA MAP P.26, POCKET MAP J12. Adliye Sok 6 🚇 1 Sultanahmet ⓦ hotelpeninsula.com. A small double here (in the semi-basement floor) is less than one in many of the city's hostels, so it's a good budget option. Newly built in traditional style, it sticks largely to the convention hereabouts of bare floor (laminate in this case), pastel walls and vaguely Ottoman-period decor. Tidy bathrooms and a range of rooms from small singles to a two-room family suite. €

SİDE HOTEL & PENSION MAP P.26, POCKET MAP H12. Utangaç Sok 20 🚇 1 Sultanahmet ⓦ sidehotel.com. Offering a choice of fairly basic and more elaborately-equipped rooms, this place has been getting good reviews since 1989 – due in no small part to the very friendly trio of brothers who run it. Rooms in the hotel section are en suite and have air conditioning, those on the pension side rely on fans for cooling. The six rooms on the upper floor have (spotless) shared bathrooms. €€

SULTAN HOSTEL MAP P.26, POCKET MAP H12. Akbıyık Cad 21 🚇 1 Sultanahmet ⓦ sultanhostel.com. The city's biggest hostel and main rival to the equally mammoth *Orient* virtually next door, it offers a wide range of rooms, from doubles to a 26-bed dorm. It's got a good reputation for cleanliness and the friendliness of its staff. Dorm rooms are good value, but you can find doubles in pensions nearby for the same, or even less, money. Dorms €, doubles €€

TURKOMAN MAP P.26, POCKET MAP G12. Asmalı Çeşme Sok 2 🚇 1 Sultanahmet ⓦ turkomanhotel.com. Right opposite the Egyptian Obelisk on the Hippodrome and housed in a tall, narrow nineteenth-century building, this long-established boutique hotel has bags of character. All the rooms have brass beds, stripped boards and high ceilings, and there's a pleasant roof terrace for breakfast, with views across to the Blue Mosque. €€

UYAN MAP P.26, POCKET MAP H12. Utangaç Sok 2 🚇 1 Sultanahmet ☎ 0212

518 9255, Ⓦ uyanhotel.com. This is one of the more stylish mid-range options in the heart of Sultanahmet, and the rooms in this converted 1920s corner-plot residence are bright, light and clean (bar ground-floor rooms) with white walls, light wood floors and crisp, white bed linen. There are good views of the Haghia Sophia from the roof terrace, while suite-room 405 is named the "Blue Mosque Room" for obvious reasons. €€

WHITE HOUSE MAP P.26, POCKET MAP G11. Çatalçeşme Sok 21 Ⓣ 1 Sultanahmet Ⓦ istanbulwhitehouse.com. On the north side of the main tramline, this beautifully appointed hotel won't suit those looking for a genuine period or boutique hotel – but it's hard to beat for reliable comfort. Rooms are faux-Ottoman, all patterned wallpapers, cream, gilt, ornate furniture and bold bedspreads. Breakfasts are excellent and views from the roof terrace are expansive. €€€

Topkapı Palace to the Golden Horn

NEORION MAP P.44, POCKET MAP G6. Orhaniye Cad 14 Ⓣ 1 Sultanahmet Ⓦ neorionhotel.com. There's nothing particularly flash about this 53-room establishment, but its staff go to considerable lengths to keep their guests happy. There is a roof terrace where you can enjoy a free drink each night while you gaze across the Bosphorus, as well as a free basement pool, jacuzzi, sauna and Turkish bath. Rooms are kept pristine, and have subtle Ottoman-style decor as well as LCD TVs. €€€

SİRKECİ MANSION MAP P.44, POCKET MAP H6. Taya Hatun Cad 5 Ⓣ 1 Gülhane Ⓦ sirkecimansion.com. Tucked away down a side street off the main tramline and overlooking the walls of Gülhane Park, this popular hotel is impeccably run. The rooms are comfortable without being overly ornate, there's a fitness centre in the basement, and nice touches like free afternoon tea and cake for guests. The roof terrace commands grand vistas over the park and Topkapı Palace beyond. €€€

Grand Bazaar and around

NILES MAP P.60, POCKET MAP E8. Dibekli Camii Sok 13 Ⓣ 1 Beyazit Ⓦ hotelniles.com. Good-value hotel on a steep street running down to the sea from the tramline and just a few minutes' walk from the Grand Bazaar. This area is more workaday than Sultanahmet, a real bonus if you want to be a little away from your fellow visitors. The standard rooms are smallish, but there's a green and pleasant patio garden plus a roof terrace with sea views. €€

PRESIDENT (RADISSON) MAP P.60, POCKET MAP E8. Tiyatro Cad 25 Ⓣ 1 Beyazit Ⓦ thepresidenthotel.com. Better-than-average large, chain hotel just minutes from the Grand Bazaar and handy for the Beyazıt tram. There's a range of different rooms, from standard doubles and twins to suites (some with sea views at a premium). Those with Sea of Marmara views carry a premium. The circular, year-round rooftop pool is a plus for some, as is the gym. €€€

The Northwest quarter

TROYA HOTEL BALAT MAP P.74, POCKET MAP C3. Abdülezelpaşa Cad 97 Ⓦ troyahotelbalat.com. The narrow, steep and twisting streets of nineteenth-century houses in up-and-coming Fener and adjoining Balat, and the Golden Horn waterfront views, make this hotel a great place to stay off the beaten track. The place oozes nineteenth-century Greek style, with original period murals in most rooms, solid wooden doors, stripped wood floors and vintage furniture. Hearty buffet breakfast too. The only drawback is traffic noise from the road running alongside the Golden Horn. €

Galata

10 KARAKÖY MAP P.86, POCKET MAP B15. Kemeraltı Cad 10 Ⓦ 10karakoy. com. This fine late nineteenth-century Neoclassical building has been given a superb makeover by renowned architect Sinan Kafadar. There's a tempting mix of standard, luxury and roof suite rooms, as well as a very sophisticated terrace bar and a slow-food-orientated dining room downstairs. €€€

ANEMON GALATA MAP P.86, POCKET MAP A15. Büyükhendek Cad 11 Ⓜ 2 Şişhane or Tünel İstiklal Ⓦ anemonhotels. com. With an excellent location on the square at the foot of the landmark Galata Tower, this place is in the heart of the district's bohemian action. The hotel itself is part of a chain, however, with mock Art Nouveau/Victoriana-style decor and maximum comfort – including tubs in the bathrooms. €€€

THE BANK HOTEL MAP P.86, POCKET MAP A15. Bankalar Cad 5, Karaköy Ⓜ 1 Karaköy or Tünel Karaköy Ⓦ thebankhotelistanbul.com. Occupying an imposing former bank building dating back to 1863, this hotel has been converted into a hotel by one of Istanbul's leading architects, Sınan Kafadar. Original features abound, including subtly patterned granite floors, high ceilings and the vaults themselves. South-facing rooms have great views over the Golden Horn, and rooms have mod-cons like big-screen LCD TVs. Part of the Marriott Bonvoy/Design Hotels brand. €€€

GEORGES HOTEL MAP P.86, POCKET MAP B14. Serdar-i Ekrem Cad 24, M2 Şişhane or Tünel Beyoğlu, Ⓦ georges. com. Well-established and immaculately run boutique hotel with a prime position on hip Serdar-I Ekrem street, sophisticated owner Alex Varlik knows his business extremely well. Stylish rooms, a superb rooftop terrace with expansive views, great food and a welcoming atmosphere. €€€

NOMAD HOSTEL MAP P.86, POCKET MAP C15. Necatibey Cad, Hoca Tahsin Sk 25 T1 Tophane Ⓦ nomadhostel.com.tr. Basic but clean and colourful hostel, well situated close to the Galata Bridge, Istanbul Modern, newly-developed Galataport area and T1 tram way for easy rides into the old city. Well-run and in the midst of a hip part of town, it's excellent value, but accommodation is in (four-bed) dorms only. €

SUB KARAKÖY MAP P.86, POCKET MAP C14. Necatibey Cad 9, Ⓦ subkarakoy. com. A very apt hotel for hip Karaköy, this stylish place with a trendy crow motif has a select number of individually designed and furnished rooms, each with a modern bathroom with rain shower and high-quality toiletries. It also has a great terrace bar with an excellent range of local wines available, as well as a wholesome whole-food breakfast which is dished-up downstairs. €€€

Beyoğlu

BÜYÜK LONDRA MAP P.96, POCKET MAP B12. Meşrutiyet Cad 117 Ⓜ 2 Şişhane or Tünel İstiklal Ⓦ londrahotel.net. The lowest priced rooms in this once extremely grand fin de siècle hotel are as cheap as you'll find in any part of the city you'd want to stay in, and despite the tiny bathrooms and slightly worn decor, they're more than adequate. The real pull here, though, is the location, time-warp bar (see page 108), roof bar and general untouched, period ambience. There's a decent breakfast too. €€

DEVMAN MAP P.96, POCKET MAP B13. Asmalımescit Sok 52 Ⓜ 2 Şişhane or Tünel İstiklal Ⓦ devmanhotel.com. Among a slew of cheapish options on bustling Asmalımescit Sokak, a narrow alley lined with meyhanes and bars, this is a great option if you're looking for basic, no-frills but clean accommodation, right in the thick of the nightlife and shopping. Can be noisy, especially on weekend nights. €

MARMARA PERA MAP P.96, POCKET MAP A13. Meşrutiyet Cad 21 Ⓜ 2 Şişhane or Tünel İstiklal Ⓦ themarmarahotels.com. A twelve-storey high-rise towering over neighbouring nineteenth-century apartment blocks and hotels, this smart establishment has stylishly modern rooms and a rooftop pool and bar with sensational views, as well as the popular Mikla restaurant (see page 107). €€€

PERA PALACE MAP P.96, POCKET MAP A13. Meşrutiyet Cad 52 Ⓜ 2 Şişhane or Tünel İstiklal Ⓦ perapalace.com. This historic hotel (see page 98) trades on its 'golden age of travel' past, so you pay a premium to stay in its refurbished rooms, but it's no worse value than many Istanbul hotels with less illustrious history. Some of its grand rooms were occupied in grander times past by the likes of Agatha Christie, Greta Garbo and Ernest Hemingway. €€€€

RICHMOND HOTEL MAP P.96, POCKET MAP B13. İstiklal Cad 227 Ⓜ 2 Şişhane or Tünel İstiklal Ⓦ richmondhotels.com.tr. Not the most stylish hotel in Beyoğlu, this is nonetheless a reliable mid-range option, with standard rooms conservatively done out in neutrals. It is well located right on İstiklal Caddesi, some upper rear rooms have great Bosphorus views (at a premium) and there's the in-house *Bistro-Urbanist* bar-restaurant (see page 109). €€

TOM TOM SUITES MAP P.96, POCKET MAP B13.Boğazkesen Cad, Tomtom Kaptan Sok 18 Ⓜ 2 Şişhane or Tünel İstiklal Ⓦ tomtomsuites.com. Located opposite the beautiful nineteenth-century Italian Consulate, this similarly dated property offers a superbly presented series of suites, all subtle whites and soft browns. It's hard to know what the Franciscan nuns who once called this place home would have made of the underfloor heated bathrooms and jacuzzis. €€€

VILLA ZURICH MAP P.96, POCKET MAP D13. Akarsu Yokuşu Cad 36, Ⓜ 2 Taksim Ⓦ hotelvillazurich.com. This is a well-established, traditional hotel located in the backstreets of now trendy Cihangir, with large, well-equipped double rooms. There's a smart rooftop terrace where you can eat a substantial breakfast while admiring the views across the Bosphorus. €€€

Beşiktaş and Ortaköy

ÇIRAĞAN PALACE KEMPİNSKİ MAP P.114. Çırağan Cad 32. Buses #25/E, #28, #40, #40/T, #42/T Ⓦ kempinski. com. As opulent as you'd imagine from a hotel fashioned from a Bosphorus-front, European-style Ottoman palace (see page 113). There's a huge outdoor pool, several restaurants and the inevitable designer boutiques. Every room has a balcony and the decor is a safe blend of the traditional and contemporary. €€€

FOUR SEASONS BOSPHORUS MAP P.114. Çırağan Cad 28. Buses #25/E, #28, #40, #40/T, #42/T Ⓦ fourseasons.com. Like rival the *Çırağan Palace Kempinski*, this upmarket chain hotel is set in a former palace on the Bosphorus and offers similar levels of comfort and luxury. The rooms and suites are very elegant and most have fabulous Bosphorus views – and there's a great pool and Turkish bath. €€€€

LES OTTOMANS MAP P.114. Muallim Naci Cad 68. Buses #25/E, #28, #40, #40/T, #42/T Ⓦ lesottomans.com. This beautiful hotel was once a grand *yalı* (waterfront mansion), but prices here make the *Four Seasons* and *Kempinski* look like budget options. This is the last word in exclusive luxury on the Bosphorus, so you probably wouldn't want to arrive here by one of the public buses listed above. €€€€

W HOTEL MAP P.114. Süleyman Seba Cad 22. Buses #25/E, #28, #40, #40/T, #42/T Ⓦ whotels.com/istanbul. Upmarket, self-consciously hip chain hotel, the *W* in Beşiktaş is appropriately set in the posh Akaretler shopping centre – no mere mall, but a series of period townhouses converted into boutiques and the like. Aimed largely at prosperous men up for some sophisticated clubbing and shopping. €€€

Bosphorus and Princes' Islands

A'JİA MAP P.128. Çubuklu Cad 27, Kanlıca Ⓦ ajiahotel.com. This is a stunningly beautiful conversion of a splendid nineteenth-century waterfront mansion house, all period charm on the outside and stylish white-is-right minimalism on the inside. The roof-rooms are the best value and have lovely little balconies overlooking the Bosphorus. €€€

ANASTASIA MEZİKİ MAP P.130. Malül Gazi Cad 24. Ferry from Kabataş Ⓦ mezikiotel.com. Set in a quiet area of Büyükada's main settlement, this turn-of-the-nineteenth-century villa oozes period charm, with original murals and furniture, and high ceilings. You'll really feel like you are stepping back in time here – especially

APARTMENTS

when you have to step out onto the landing at night to use the shared bathrooms. €€

MEHTAP 45 MAP P.130. Burgazada. Ferry from Eminönü or Kadıköy ☎ 0216 381 2660. Quiet island, quiet boutique-style hotel with grand views across the Sea of Marmara back to the metropolis. Plain, simple but comfy rooms, but note that here, and at most Princes' Island hotels, you pay a fifty percent premium for Saturday-night stays. €€

PRENSET PANSİYON MAP P.130. Ayyıldız Cad 40–42/A, Heybeliada. Ferry from Eminönü or Kadıköy ☎ 0216 351 0039. Cheap and cheerful pension close to the ferry terminal and in the middle of the village close to all the restaurants and cafés. Few rooms have good views. €

SPLENDID PALAS MAP P.130. Nisan Cad 23, Büyükada. Ferry from Eminönü or Kadıköy ⓦ splendidhotel.net. A grand, white-painted wooden *fin de siècle* hotel, complete with cupolas and balconies, this period gem once hosted Edward VIII and Mrs Simpson. There's a pool out back and great sea views from the front rooms. €€€

SUMAHAN ON THE WATER MAP P.128. Kuleli Cad 43, Cengelköy ⓦ sumahan. com. A distillery converted into an award-winning hotel right on the Asian side of the Bosphorus, in the attractive suburb of Cengelköy. This very stylish place blends the traditional and the modern with verve and makes an ideal retreat from the city hubbub. €€€€

Apartments

Apartments are becoming popular in Istanbul, even for short breaks. With some exceptions, they tend to be concentrated in Galata and Beyoğlu and are often part of a converted period townhouse. Good websites include ⓦ cross-pollinate.com, which offers a wide range of apartments suited to all budgets, mainly in Beyoğlu and Galata. Below are a few recommended apartments, with prices given for one-night, high-season stays.

ISTANBUL HUB FLATS Kocatepe, Taksim Çeşmesi Sok 9, Beyoğlu ☎ 0532 316 2238. Two well-equipped apartments in a block in Taksim, one of them a duplex. Neither apartment is either uber-cool or dripping with period charm, but rates are very reasonable – though considerably higher if you opt for a free cancellation booking. Easily bookable online via various accommodation booking providers. €€

PASHA Serdar-I Ekrem Cad, Galata Tünel İstiklal ⓦ istanbulplace.com. Looking south across the Golden Horn, the sitting room and main bedroom of this beautifully restored nineteenth-century apartment have great old city skyline views. There are three good-sized bedrooms, a stylish kitchen and a separate shower room. Perfect combination

of period features and contemporary white decor and furnishings. €€€

ROOMS GALATA Kumbarcı Yokuşu 37 ⓦ roomsgalata.com. Sixteen cool rooms in a beautiful period house, linked by a swish spiral staircase. Kitchenettes, and king, queen or single beds. €€

Letting agencies

BLUEGROUND ISTANBUL
ⓦ theblueground.com. A range of well-furnished and equipped serviced apartments to rent across the city, including the areas most popular with visitors such as Kadıköy, Beşiktaş and Beyoğlu, although they have nothing to let in the old city. Minimum rental one month.

ISTANBUL!PLACE APARTMENTS Galata ⓦ istanbulplace.com. Anglo-Turkish-run company offering ten beautifully restored period townhouse apartments in and around Galata.

MANZARA İSTANBUL Tatarbeyi Sok 26b, Galata ⓦ manzara-apartments.com. Run by a German-born Turkish architect, this company has forty quality properties, mainly in Galata and Beyoğlu.

ESSENTIALS

Cross-Bosphorus ferry

Arrival

The vast majority of foreign visitors reach Istanbul by air, though there are good road links and rather less useful rail connections with the rest of Europe. The city is also a major stop on Mediterranean cruises.

By plane

Istanbul has two major airports, Istanbul Airport (ⓦ istairport.com) on the European side of the city, and Sabiha Gökçen (ⓦ sgairport.com) across the Bosphorus in Asia. The former, one of the world's busiest airports, is used mainly by scheduled airlines; the latter, further from the city centre, by budget European carriers.

Istanbul Airport

Located some 40km northwest of the city centre, the airport is linked to Aksaray/Beyzıt (for Sultanahmet and the old city) and Taksim (for Beyoğlu and Galata) by Havaist (ⓦ hava.ist. com) shuttle buses, which run every 30 minutes, 24 hours a day (₺113). The journey takes between 45 minutes and one and a half hours depending on traffic. It is much cheaper to use the metro system (₺22), but more complicated, as it means taking the M11 line to Kagıthane, then the M7 line to Mecidiyeköy and finally the M2 line to Şişhane (the last is in

Beyoğlu/Galata). The journey time should also be around 45 minutes. It is also possible to use IETT (ⓦ iett. istanbul) buses H-1, H2, H3 and H6, but the stops are inconvenient for most visitors. For all but the Havist buses buy an Istanbulkart (see box, below) from the blue/yellow machines near the exit of the arrival floors. A taxi to Sultanahmet will cost around ₺460.

Sabiha Gökçen Airport

Havaist buses run half-hourly to Kadıköy (Asian side of the Bosphorus) between 4.15am and 9.15pm (₺50) and Taksim (for Beyoğlu and onto the old city) half hourly between 3.30am and 10pm (₺67.5). It's also possible to take the M4 metro from the airport to Kadiköy (₺12); connect to the old city by taking a cross continent ferry from Kadiköy (ⓦ sehirhatlari.istanbul) to Eminönü or Karaköy (₺12); ferries approximately every 20 minutes from 6.10am to midnight. You can use the Istanbulkart travel pass for both. Taxis to Sultanahmet cost about ₺670.

By train

Reaching Istanbul by train today is far from the pleasure it must have been in the Orient Express days and is only for the patient and committed rail buff. The most straightforward

Istanbulkart

This contactless credit-card-sized smartcard can be used on buses, the metro and tram, ferries and sea buses, plus the funiculars. It can be purchased from machines and kiosks near major transport stops, including at both international airports, and can also be topped-up in these places. The official price is ₺50, but kiosk vendors usually add a small ₺2 mark-up. Unlike many other travel smartcards, this card can be used by multiple passengers, so you only need to purchase one card. The amount deducted from the card varies according to the mode of transport – for example a bus, tram or metro trip is ₺9.9, ferries ₺12.5, or ferries to the Princes' Islands ₺28.7.

route from London is via Paris, Munich, Vienna, Budapest and Bucharest. From Bucharest, a train runs to Dimitrovgrad in Bulgaria. Change to the Bosfor Ekspresi, which runs between Sofia and Istanbul, for onward travel to Halkalı, a suburban station some 16km west of central Istanbul. From Halkalı take the Marmaray metro to Sirkeci for Sultanahmet/old city. For the best information, see rail enthusiasts' delight ⓦseat61.com.

By bus

Coaches run by several Turkish companies link Istanbul to other European cities. Ulusoy (ⓦulusoy. com.tr) has buses to eleven German cities, while Metro (ⓦmetroturizm. com.tr) runs coaches to Athens, Sofia and Georgia. Buses arrive at Esenler otogar (bus station), linked to the city centre by the M1 metro – switch to the T1 tram at Aksaray. Buses from all Turkish destinations also terminate at Esenler, though some also stop at Harem on the Asian side of the Bosphorus, from where regular ferries cross the strait to Eminönü.

By sea

Cruise ships dock at recently completed (2022) Galataport, a swish complex of shops and eating places as well as the cruise ship terminal, on the north side of the Golden Horn not far northeast of the Galata Bridge, from where it's a short walk to the Karaköy T1 tram stop (for Sultanahmet) or the Tünel (for Galata/Beyoğlu).

Getting around

It's fortunate that, despite Istanbul's huge sprawl, most areas of interest are close enough to explore on foot. Judicious use of the city's metro, tram, bus and ferry network will, however, enable you to get to slightly out of the way places and save your legs. Although it is certainly possible to buy single (and multiple) tickets from Biletix machines, it does not make sense as you will pay double for the privilege. It's far better to purchase an Istanbulkart (see box, page 144), which makes your journey cheaper and transition between the various forms of transport much smoother.

Buses and dolmuşes

Buses are the most daunting of Istanbul's public transport options, as visitors often find it difficult to know which one to get on or where to get off – plus they can be uncomfortably crowded. Having said that, they are a cheap way of getting around and reach places other modes of transport (bar taxis) don't. **Municipality buses** are labelled IETT (Istanbul Elektrik Tramway ve Tünel) though there are some private ones. Most run daily 6.30am–11pm. The most useful bus stations in the old city are Beyazıt, Edirnekapı and Eminönü, across the Golden Horn Taksim Square and Kabataş, and there are several routes that may be useful for visitors (see box, page 146). **Dolmuşes** are a kind of shared taxi (either a car or minibus), but the only really useful routes are the yellow minibuses departing the Taksim end of Tarlabaşı Bulvarı for the old city and Yedikule (see page 77) or connecting Kadıköy and Üsküdar in Asia. Note that you'll need cash for these.

Trams

The most useful transport route for visitors is the T1 tramline, which runs from Bağcılar in the west to the ferry terminal/bus station and funicular at Kabataş, on the north side of the

Useful bus routes

For information in English on the bus network in Istanbul, check ⓦ iett.istanbul/en, although it's a bit tricky to use. On the home page click on the route planner for details of routes, stops and maps.

Istanbul in Asia

#12 and **#12/A** Kadıköy to Üsküdar

#15 Üsküdar along the Bosphorus to Beylerbeyi, Kanlıca and Beykoz

#15/A Beykoz to Anadolu Kavağı

European Istanbul

#22 Kabataş along the Bosphorus to İstiniye via Beşiktaş, Ortaköy, Arnavutköy, Bebek and Emirgan

#25/A Haciosman metro to Rumeli Kavağı via Tarabya and Sariyer

#25/E Kabataş to Sariyer via Beşiktaş, Ortaköy, Arnavutköy, Bebek and Emirgan

#28 Beşiktaş to Edirnekapı via Eminönü Transit and Fatih (for Fatih and Yavuz Selim mosques, land walls and Kariye Mosque)

#28/T Beşiktaş to Topkapı via Karaköy, Eminönü Transit and Fatih

#36/V and **#37/Y** Vezneciler to Edirnekapı via Fatih (for Fatih and Yavuz Selim mosques, land walls and Kariye Mosque)

#38/E Eminönü to Edirnekapı via Unkapanı Bridge and Fatih (for Fatih and Yavuz Selim mosques, land walls and Kariye Museum)

#38 Beyazıt to Edirnekapı via Aksaray (for Historia Mall, Akdeniz Hatay Sofrası, land walls, Kariye Museum)

#40 Taksim to Sariyer via Beşiktaş, Ortaköy, Arnavutköy, Bebek and Emirgan

#55/EB Beyazıt to Eyüp via Aksaray, Fatih and Edirnekapı (for Yavuz Selim mosque, land walls, Kariye Museum and *Pierre Loti* café)

#54/HT Taksim to upper Golden Horn (for Miniatürk, Rahmi M. Koç Industrial Museum and Santralistanbul)

#80/T Taksim to Yedikule (for south end of land walls)

#87 Taksim to Edirnekapı via Fatih (for Fatih and Yavuz Selim mosques, land walls and Kariye Museum)

#99 Eminönü along Golden Horn (for Fener, Balat, north end of land walls, Eyüp and Santralistanbul)

Golden Horn. It heads through the old city, with stops including the Grand Bazaar, Sultanahmet, Sirkeci, Eminönü (for ferries to Asia), Karaköy (for ferries to Asia and Galata and the Tünel to Beyoğlu) and Kabataş (for the funicular to Taksim and buses along the European shore of the Bosphorus). The so-called **antique tram** (daily 9am–9pm, ₺9.90) rumbles up and down İstiklal Caddesi from Tünel İstiklal to Taksim Square.

Metro

There are several lines but only the M1, M2, M7, M11 and Marmaray lines will be of use to the majority of visitors. The M1 metro is useful for getting out to the land walls reasonably close to the Kariye Mosque (see page 72). The M2 metro runs from Yenikapı in the old city north across the Golden Horn to Şişhane at the southern end of İstiklal Caddesi. From there, it runs north again to Taksim and out to the suburbs. The

Marmaray line runs from Halkalı in the west (Europe) via Kazlıçesme (useful for the southern terminus of the land walls of Theodosius) eastwards to Yenikapı (where it connects with the M2 metro) then to Sirkeci, under the Bosphorus to Üsküdar, on to Ayrılık Çeşmesi, where it connects to the M4 metro for Kadıköy, and to Gebze. The M7 and M11 metros are only useful to the vast majority of visitors for the trip to and from Istanbul Airport.

Funiculars

The F1 funicular links the transport hub at Kabataş with Taksim Square, while the nineteenth-century funicular, the **Tünel** (7am–10pm; ₺15 or ₺9.90 with Istanbulkart), connects Karaköy on the Golden Horn with Beyoğlu/Istiklal Caddesi at the top of the hill. There's also a **cable car** (₺15 or 9.90 with Istanbulkart) linking the shores of the Golden Horn at Eyüp with the cemetery and *Pierre Loti* café (see page 82).

Ferries

Few will want to visit Istanbul and not take a ferry ride to Asia and/or up the Bosphorus or Golden Horn. Şehir Hatları (ⓦ sehirhatlari.istanbul) is the main company – make sure you pick up a timetable from a ferry terminal or tourist office as times do change,

or check their website. The main city terminal is at Eminönü, just east of the Galata Bridge, from where ferries run across the Bosphorus to Kadıköy (daily 6.40am–9.10pm; ₺9.90) and Üsküdar (daily 6.40am–11pm; ₺9.90) around three to five times an hour (they are primarily for commuters). The terminal for the Şehir Hatları Bosphorus Cruise (see page 82) is also here. To the west of the bridge, from Yemiş İskele, Haliç Hattı ferries originating from Üsküdar run (approximately hourly) up the Golden Horn to Eyüp, which is useful for visits to the Rahmi M. Koç Industrial Museum (see page 82), the northern end of the land walls. From Karaköy, across the Galata Bridge, there are ferries to Kadıköy (6.35am–midnight; ₺9.90). Princes' Islands run mainly from Kabataş, stopping at Kadıköy en route, from 6.45am to 11.30pm. A number of smaller private companies also operate boats across the Bosphorus and to the Princes' Islands, notably Turyol, with boats departing to Asia from terminals just west of the Galata Bridge on both sides of the Golden Horn.

Taxis

Yellow taxis are ubiquitous and are very useful when visiting out-of-the-way sights and – assuming the

Transport infrastructure projects

The Marmaray transport infrastructure project includes a rail tunnel under the Bosphorus linking European and Asian Istanbul. The tunnel finally opened in 2013 after years of delays caused by the uncovering of archeological finds while digging the Yenikapı hub. From Yenikapı, the line runs to Sirkeci, then to Üsküdar and west to Halkalı. In 2014 the construction of a controversial bridge across the Golden Horn allowed the M2 to link with the Marmaray line. The Yavuz Sultan Selim Bridge, a third one across the Bosphorus carrying road and rail traffic, opened in 2016. Later the same year a new road tunnel opened under the river, linking Kazlıçeşme in Europe with Harem in Asia. Construction of Canal Istanbul, originally slated to commence in 2019, is now set to be completed in 2027.

driver is honest – reasonably cheap (a standing charge of ₺14.55, then ₺9.79 per km). Make sure the meter is turned on before setting off – ensuring the driver follows the shortest route is trickier. One way to avoid potential disputes is to get your hotel to arrange a taxi for you for an agreed price.

Tourist buses

Hop On Hop Off Istanbul (⊕ hoponhopoffistanbul.com) has a hop-on, hop-off service (full tour 2h 30 min) with a recorded guide. Departures are from either opposite the Haghia Sophia or across the Golden Horn in Taksim. Buses leave half hourly between 10am and 5pm and take in the old city, the Golden Horn and Asian side of the Bosphorus. Tickets cost ₺1,186.

Walking and special interest tours

Istanbul Walks (⊕ istanbulwalks. com) offers guided walks of the city that include all the major historic sites (admission not included), starting at around ₺2,000 for a half day. More specialist is **Fest Travel** (⊕ festtravel.com), which offers a wide range of strolls around quarters of the city where it's easy to miss the most interesting sights if you are on your own, making this great for discovering unusual angles on Istanbul. **Istanbul Tour Studio** (⊕ istanbultourstudio.com) offer a range of activities including sailing, rowing on the Golden Horn, cycling in Asia and exploring the city's street art scene.

Directory A–Z

Accessible Travel

The good news is that the useful T1 tram is reasonably easy to access, and will save time and effort pushing a wheelchair along busy Divan Yolu. The metro has few accessible stations. Buses have ramps and low doors, but are so crowded that using them is tricky, especially given the language barrier, and they are not allowed into Sultanahmet. The Topkapı Palace (see page 43), Haghia Sophia (see page 25) and Archeology Museum (see page 42) are partly accessible by wheelchair, as is the Blue Mosque (see page 34). Unfortunately, the old city's steep streets and cobbled surfaces can make it difficult to

get around between sights, and few mosques allow wheelchairs. Despite friendly and helpful staff, many other museums and sights do not have wheelchair access, with the honourable exceptions of the Rahmi M. Koç Industrial Museum (see page 88), Istanbul Modern (see page 87) and the Pera Museum (see page 98).

Cinema

Most films are screened in the language in which they were shot, with Turkish subtitles for non-Turkish productions. The exceptions are children's films, which are generally dubbed into Turkish. There are several cinemas on or just off İstiklal Caddesi

Emergency numbers

Ambulance ☏ 112
Fire ☏ 110
Police ☏ 155
Traffic Police ☏ 154

Security threats

Due in no small part to fear over terrorist attacks, Turkey has suffered periodic drops in tourist numbers. There were several high-profile attacks in 2016, and in the early hours of 2017 a gunman killed 39 at *Reina* nightclub. In November 2022, six people were killed in a bombing on major city thoroughfare, Istiklal Caddesi. Airport-style security has been introduced at major tourist attractions in Istanbul, and safety measures have been tightened city-wide. Stay well away from demonstrations and be sure to consult the latest government travel advice ahead of time, and you're likely to enjoy a safe visit.

between Galatasaray Meydanı and Taksim Square (see page 99), the largest of which is Cinemaximum Fitaş (ⓦ intersinema.com), and there's one in Sultanahmet, the Şafak (ⓦ ozenfilm. com.tr). Otherwise, head to one of the big shopping malls. Tickets from ₺95.

Consulates
Australia Asker Ocağı Cad 15, Elmadağ, Şişli ☎ 0212 393 8542.
Canada Tekfen Tower, 209 Büyükdere Cad, Levent 4 ☎ 0212 272 5174.
New Zealand İnönü Cad 48/3, Taksim ☎ 0212 244 0272.
South Africa (Honorary Consul) Alarko Centre, Muallim Naci Cad 113–115, Ortaköy ☎ 0212 260 378.
UK Meşrutiyet Cad 34, Tepebaşı, Beyoğlu ☎ 0212 334 6400.
US Kaplıcalar Mevkii Sok 2, İstinye ☎ 0212 335 9000.

Crime
Mugging and assaults are rare, though pickpocketing is increasingly common – take care on the crowded transport system. Be wary of Taksim Square at night, notably where it joins Tarlabaşı Bulvarı, and the land walls at dusk/evening time. There are several police forces in Turkey but the branch you're most likely to require is the Security Police (Emniyet Polisi), recognized by their blue shirts. The Tourist Police (Turizm Polisi) have a station, open 24hr, at Yerebatan Cad 6 (☎ 0212 527

4503). Blue-uniformed Market Police (Zabitas) patrol commercial areas.

Electricity
Voltage is 220–240 AC, 50Hz, using standard continental-European two round-pin plugs, so bring an adaptor if necessary.

Entry requirements
Make sure you have a full passport with at least six months' validity. Citizens of the UK, Ireland and New Zealand do not require a visa to enter Turkey and can stay up to 90 days in any 180 day period. Citizens of Australia, Canada and the US require a visa, which allows multiple entry and stays of up to 90 days. Visas are available in advance from ⓦ evisa.gov.tr, and for citizens of the US cost $50, or $60 for Australia and Canada. Note that entry requirements change; consult the Turkish Ministry of Foreign Affairs at ⓦ mfa.gov.tr for the latest regulations.

Health
For minor complaints visit a pharmacy (*eczane*). Many pharmacists speak English and most antibiotics are available without a prescription. Pharmacies open 9am–7pm Mon–Sat but there is always a night duty pharmacy (*nöbetçi eczane*) open 24hr including Sundays – the address of the nearest is posted in pharmacy windows.

Both public and private hospitals are well equipped, but state hospitals are often overcrowded and run-down. Private establishments usually have more English-speaking doctors and often a designated translator. Facilities are generally top notch and they are well-used to dealing with foreign private patients (and relieving them of their cash – make sure you're insured).

The Taksim First Aid Hospital (Taksim İlkyardim Hastanesi) at Sıraselviler Cad 112, Taksim (☎ 0212 252 4300), is state-run and only treats emergencies. The private American Hospital (Amerikan Hastanesi, Güzelbahçe Sok 20, Nişantaşı, ☎ 0212 311 2000, ⓦ amerikanhastanesi.org), is state-of-the-art and also has a dental clinic. The International Hospital (İstanbul Cad 82, Yeşilköy, ☎ 0212 468 4444, ⓦ internationalhospital.com.tr), has a full range of medical services and 24-hour emergency care. For a regular rather than hospital dentist, Prodent (Can Ergene) at Valikonağı Cad 109/5, Nişantaşı (☎ 0212 230 4635), is reliable and English-speaking. Dental care is generally both excellent and relatively cheap in Turkey.

Internet

Virtually every hostel, pension and hotel in Istanbul offers free wi-fi and often a fixed terminal or two as well. Many upmarket cafés also have free wi-fi, especially those situated in Galata and Beyoğlu. Internet cafes are on the decline, but a few remain scattered around the city.

Left luggage

There are lockers at both Istanbul and Sabiha Gökçen airports (₺155 for 24hr).

LGBTQ+ travellers

Istanbul has a very active LGBTQ+ scene despite the ambivalence of Turkish society to homosexuality. The scene is centred largely on Taksim and Beyoğlu, where there are a number of LGBTQ+ cafés and clubs. Istanbul Pride, an annual parade from Taksim Square along Istiklal Caddesi, has been subject to prohibition orders and police crackdowns in recent years, a sign of a new conservatism in Turkish politics. For more information on LGBTQ+ Istanbul see ⓦ istanbulgay.com or, for gay-friendly accommodation, check ⓦ gayhomestays.com/top-destinations/Istanbul.

Lost property

For anything lost (or stolen) contact the Tourist Police at Yerebatan Cad 6 (☎ 0212 527 4503) in Sultanahmet.

Money

Turkey's currency is the Turkish lira (Türk lirası), TL for short, divided into smaller units known as kuruş. Prices are displayed as either 25TL, for example, or using the symbol ₺. Coins come in denominations of 1, 5, 10, 25, 50 kuruş and 1 lira, with notes in denominations of 5, 10, 20, 50, 100 and 200 lira. At the time of writing, the ₺ symbol was being used by businesses either in front of the numerical figure or after it; although officially it should be placed before. High inflation has resulted in the Turkish lira deflating massively against many foreign currencies in recent years, and prices quoted in lira can soon be out of date.

There are many, many ATMs throughout the city. All have touch-screen English options, those in major tourist areas dispense euros and dollars as well as Turkish lira. Many banks will change money, but they can be slow and cumbersome – for the best rate use the state-owned Ziraat Bankası (Mon–Fri 8.30am–noon & 1.30pm–5pm), which has a dedicated exchange counter and an automated queuing system. You can also change money at the Post Office (PTT) commission-free and at a reasonable rate. The other alternative is an exchange bureau (döviz bürosu). The rate is usually slightly less than the Ziraat Bankası, but the procedure much quicker, and opening hours are longer (generally Mon–Sat 9am–8pm) than banks. There are several around the Sultanahmet tram-stop area on Divan Yolu as well as on İstiklal Caddesi. Credit cards are widely accepted in most tourist-orientated hotels and upmarket restaurants but sometimes attract a surcharge.

Mosque essentials

Turkey is ninety-nine percent Muslim, and although Istanbul is a vibrant, cosmopolitan city, many of its inhabitants take their religion seriously, so it pays to be respectful when visiting mosques. The basic rules of entry are:
Cover your head (women) and shoulders and upper arms (men and women).
No shorts (either sex) or miniskirts
Take off shoes before entering (often a plastic bag is provided for you to place your shoes in and carry around; alternatively, place them on one of the shelves provided).

Friday midday prayers are the most important of the week and visiting

at this time is not advised – indeed, visiting at any of the five daily prayer times is best avoided, though in most cases you will not cause offence. Don't speak too loudly (there are often people in the mosque either praying or learning the Koran) and don't point your camera at worshippers. Mosques always have a donation box which you may want to contribute to. Take note that there are no set opening and closing times and many of the big mosques in the old city will be open all day, from first to last prayer call (which varies through the year according to sunrise and sunset). Smaller mosques in more out of the way places are often kept locked outside prayer times and you may need to track down the caretaker or imam.

Museum passes

Five-day Istanbul Museum passes can be both cost and time effective. The pass (₺2,250) gives entry to Haghia Sophia, Haghia Eirene, Galata Mevlevî Lodge, Fethiye Museum, Topkapı Palace and Harem, the Archeological Museum, the Mosaic Museum, and the Museum of Turkish and Islamic Art and History of Science and Technology in Islam Museum, a substantial saving on individual entries. The pass allows fast-track entry to sites – useful as Haghia Sophia and Topkapı often have interminable queues. Possession of the pass also gives discounted entry to several other museums in the city. Passes are available from some of the museums, or online as an e-ticket from Ⓦ muze.gov.tr.

Opening hours

Although in Turkey state-run museums invariably close on a Monday, some in Istanbul buck this rule, so make sure you check the opening days of a particular place before visiting. Opening hours are often 9am–7pm between April and October, and 9am–5pm from November to March, but many have the same opening hours year-round. Private museums follow the same general opening hours as their state-run cousins but sometimes shut for lunch. Banks and government offices usually open Mon–Fri 8.30am–noon and 1.30–5pm. Shop opening hours vary widely, with most opening from between 9am or 10am to 7pm, but many more, especially in Beyoğlu, stay open until 9 or 10pm. *Bakkals*, small general stores, and kiosks selling papers, gum, tissues etc are often open from 7am–10pm. The Grand Bazaar is open Mon–Sat 9am–7pm, modern malls usually 10am–10pm seven days a week. For mosques see Mosque Essentials (see page 151).

Phones

Note that Istanbul has two codes, 0212 for the European side of the city, 0216 for the Asian. Turkey's country code is 90, directory enquiries 118, and 115 for the international operator. To phone overseas, purchase an international calling card, the best of which is the Alocard, available from post offices (PTT) and usable at public phones – just dial the access number supplied with the card, scratch to reveal the 12-digit PIN and enter it, then dial the overseas number. A ₺10 card allows over 1hr 15min of calling time to the UK or US. There are plenty of public phone booths scattered around the city, often outside major transport hubs such as Sirkeci, and also at PTTs. Assuming you have a roaming facility your mobile will connect with one of the local providers, though US phones won't work here. Calls are predictably expensive, around £1.30 per minute to the UK, plus you pay for incoming calls. Buying a local SIM card is a reasonable option if you are planning staying in Istanbul/Turkey for more than a week or wish to use it

frequently. The three main providers (Türkcell, AVEA and Vodaphone) have outlets at both Istanbul and Sabiha Gökçen airports, where you must complete a registration form and have your passport photocopied. A typical pay-as-you-go package is ₺674. After 120 days your phone will be blocked for use with the Turkish SIM.

Post

The two main post offices (PTT) are the massive Sirkeci PTT on Büyük Postane Caddesi, Eminönü (daily 8.30am–7pm; ☎ 0212 526 1200), and at Yeniçarşısı Caddesi, Beyoğlu (Mon–Fri & Sun 8.30am–5.30pm; ☎ 0212 444 1788), just off Galatasaray Meydanı.

Smoking

Smoking is banned on public transport and in all indoor places, although the ban is widely flouted in some bars and traditional teahouses. Many bars, cafés and restaurants get around the ban by providing outside or courtyard tables, which are covered with plastic and/or warmed with heaters in winter. The rule also applies to *nargile* (water pipe) cafés.

Time

Turkey is two hours ahead of GMT in summer, and three in winter. There is no am/pm in Turkey, which uses the 24-hour clock.

Tipping

A ten to fifteen percent service charge is standard in fancy restaurants, though as this goes to the establishment, you should tip the waiters a further five percent. Waiters in basic establishments will also appreciate the same.

Toilets

In heavily touristed parts of the city there are sufficient public toilets, in less-visited parts like the land walls and northwest quarter far fewer. Virtually all mosques have toilets attached. At both public and mosque toilets you have to pay a small fee, and note that they are invariably of the squat variety and provide no paper. Bars, cafés, restaurants and hotels all have western-style toilets.

Tourist information

There are six tourist offices (bit.ly/IstanbulTourism) across the city. The most central is at Divan Yolu 3, Sultanahmet (daily 9am–5pm; ☎ 0212 518 8754) near the Haghia Sophia, which has English-speaking staff and maps. There's also an office at Sirkeci station (daily 9am–5pm; ☎ 0212 511 5888). Across the Golden Horn in Taksim head for the office at AKM Yani (daily 10am–5pm). There are also offices at both international airports; Istanbul Airport (daily 10am–7pm; ☎ 0212 891 6205) and Sabiha Gökçen (daily 10am–7pm; ☎ 0216 588 8764).

Travelling with children

While there are few specifically child-friendly sights in Istanbul, and it can appear dauntingly crowded and hectic at times, most kids will find Istanbul an absorbing place to visit. The boat rides up and down the Bosphorus, across to Asia and out to the Princes' Islands are all great fun with kids, and several of the city's museums and galleries will be of interest. The Military Museum (see page 101) may be a little stuffy but has enough weaponry to keep kids of a certain age quiet for a while, as will the detailed scale models in Miniatürk (see page 89). Then there are the hands-on science machines at Santralistanbul (see page 89) and the plethora of vintage modes of transport and more at the Rahmi Koç Industrial Museum – plus the life-like panorama of the 1453 siege of Constantinople at the Panorama 1453 Museum (see page 79). Both Gülhane Park (see page 48) and Yıldız Park (see page 115) have plenty of green and open space for kids to run off some energy. Turks love kids, the family means everything here and cafés and restaurants are usually very tolerant of them.

Turkish baths (hamam)

Essentially a continuation of the Roman tradition, the Ottoman Turks made the hamam a central feature of everyday life and they were often attached to the great imperial mosque complexes such as the Süleymaniye (see page 58). Today the importance of the hamam has declined significantly, though they are still used by locals to relax and meet up with friends. For many visitors the hamam experience is a must, especially in Istanbul as it boasts many historic hamams, worth seeing for their architecture alone. Some have separate sections for men and women, others are segregated according to a schedule. The vast majority have a foyer/changing area, often with a café, and somewhere to leave your valuables. The main event is the steamy, domed *hararet*, where bathers soap-up and sluice themselves with water of varying degrees of hot and cold, or lie on the *göbek taşı* or navel stone, a raised and heated marble platform in the centre of the room. There is a basic charge for this self-service bath, the traditional scrub and massage are extra. Detailed information on individual hamams is given in the relevant Places chapters; in the old city the Ayasofya Hürrem Sultan (see page 30), Cağaloğlu (see page 49), Çemberlitaş (see page 63) and Süleymaniye (see page 59); in Tophane the Kılıç Ali Paşa (see page 88), in Beyoğlu the Galatasaray Hamamı (see page 100); and in Üsküdar the Çinili (see page 118).

Festivals and events

Public holidays are denoted by PH and banks, schools and government offices close on these days, though most private businesses, including cafés and restaurants, stay open, and all transport runs as normal. Tickets for many events can be bought online from ⓦ biletix.com and ⓦ pozitif.com. For more information visit ⓦ iksv.org/eng or ask in one of the city tourist offices. Note that the dates of many festivals and events are not finalised until very late, so check websites for details.

New Year's Day (PH)

January 1

Istanbul Film Festival

April ⓦ film.iksv.org

Twelve-day film festival featuring a decent mix of domestic and foreign flicks. This is a good chance to see some of the best new Turkish films with English subtitles.

Tulip Festival

Mid-April to mid-May

Over fifteen million tulip bulbs planted across the city bloom at this time, and there are plenty of associated celebrations. The most convenient places to see Turkey's national flower are Gülhane, Yıldız and Emirgan parks.

Children's Day (PH)

April 23

A celebration of Turkish independence and Turkey's children, school-band marches take place across the city, notably on İstiklal Caddesi.

Youth and Sports Day (PH)

May 19

Marches and celebrations on the anniversary of the day Atatürk launched the Turkish War of Independence.

International Theatre Festival

Mid-May to early June ⓦ iksv.org

Major festival featuring Turkish and foreign theatre companies performing in venues such as the Rumeli Hisarı fortress on the Bosphorus.

Chill-Out

May ⓦ chilloutfest.com

Weekend-long dance, electronic and pop festival held at Life Park.

Conquest Celebrations

May 29 ⓦ ibb.gov.tr

Week of festivities to mark the date of the fall of Constantinople to the Ottoman Turks, with concerts by the military Mehter Band, parades and fireworks.

Istanbul Music Festival

Mid-June to mid-July ⓦ muzik.iksv.org

Lasting most of the month, concerts, dance and opera are performed at some interesting venues by a mix of Turkish and international performers.

Istanbul Jazz Festival

First two weeks of July ⓦ caz.iksv.org

Music – not all of it is jazz – played at a series of venues across the city.

Victory Day (PH)

August 30

Celebrates the victory of the Turks over the invading Greeks at the Battle of Dumlupınar in 1922.

Contemporary Istanbul

September ⓦ contemporaryistanbul.com

This is a major, week-long arts fair based in the prestigious Lütfi Kırdar Congress and Exhibition Centre.

World Food Istanbul

September ⓦ worldfood-istanbul.com

A three-day festival celebrating Turkey's rich culinary heritage as well

Religious holidays

The religious festivals observed throughout the Islamic world also apply to Istanbul. **Ramazan** (Ramadan), the period of fasting for the month preceding **Şeker Bayramı** (Eid ul Fitr in Arabic) is not a holiday, but if your visit coincides with this month you may notice that some cafés and restaurants, especially away from the tourist haunts, are unusually quiet in the day, and packed with fast-breakers after sunset. Try to avoid eating and drinking too obviously in front of people in conservative areas like Fatih (northwest quarter). Şeker Bayramı is usually a three-day festival, with banks, government offices and many private businesses closed for the entire period, though transport continues to run. Museums are usually shut only on the first day of the holiday.

Kurban Bayramı (Eid ul Adha in Arabic) is a four-day festival during which animals are slaughtered to commemorate Abraham sacrificing a ram instead of his son. The same rules regarding closures apply as for Şeker Bayramı. As the Muslim calendar is lunar, the festivals occur eleven days earlier each year.

Şeker Bayramı	Kurban Bayramı
2024 April 9-10	2024 June 16-20
2025 March 30-31	2025 June 6-10
2026 March 19-20	2026 May 26-30
2027 March 9-10	2027 May 16-20

as world cuisine, held at the TUYAP Congress centre.

International Istanbul Biennial

Mid-September to mid-November
Ⓦ bienal.iksv.org
Held in even years in venues across the city, next up in 2024, this is a major contemporary arts event.

Republic Day (PH)

October 29
Street parade by schoolchildren to mark the foundation of the Turkish Republic on this day in 1923.

Akbank International Jazz Festival

First three weeks in October/November
Ⓦ akbanksanat.com
Quality jazz festival with leading domestic and foreign artists performing at venues such as Babylon, İKSV Salon and the Lütfi Kırdar Congress Centre.

Istanbul Marathon

November Ⓦ maraton.istanbul
The world's only trans-continental marathon causes delight for runners and spectators alike as road closures force Istanbul's notoriously heavy traffic to stay home.

Atatürk's Death (PH)

November 10
The founder of the Republic died at the Dolmabahçe Palace on this day in 1938. At 9.05am, the time of his death, people throughout the city and country stop what they are doing and observe a five-minute respectful silence.

Istanbul Short Film Festival

Mid-December
Ⓦ istanbulfilmfestival.com
During this festival over a thousand short films from Turkey and around the world are screened in cinemas across the city.

Chronology

c.6500 BC Neolithic human settlement on the site of Istanbul.

c.667 BC The legendary foundation of Byzantium (Istanbul) by Greek colonists led by Byzas.

513 BC Darius, King of Persia, captures Byzantium.

334 BC Alexander the Great captures Byzantium.

195 AD Roman emperor Septimius Severus burns the city to the ground, then proceeds to rebuild it a few years later.

324 Emperor Constantine decides the city will be his new imperial capital, building starts.

330 Constantine calls the rebuilt city Nova Roma, but it's soon known as Constantinople.

337 Constantine is baptized a Christian.

392 Paganism is banned by Emperor Theodosius and the Roman Empire becomes overtly Christian.

447 The city walls are rebuilt following a massive earthquake which destroyed much of the city.

532 The Nika riots cause vast damage to the city before 30,000 of the rioters are massacred in the Hippodrome.

537 A monumental new cathedral, the Haghia Sophia (Aya Sofya) is completed on the site of an earlier incarnation that was burned in the 532 riots.

674 The Arabs besiege Constantinople; the defenders use "Greek fire" against their enemy.

726 Emperor Leo III forbids icon veneration as idolatry, causing riots across the empire.

1054 Schism of the Orthodox and Catholic churches.

1071 The first Turks reach Anatolia and defeat Emperor Romanos IV Diogenes at Manzikert.

1097 The First Crusade passes through Constantinople.

1204 The Fourth Crusade captures Constantinople and irrevocably weakens the Byzantine Empire.

1261 Michael VIII Palaeologus recaptures the city for the Byzantines.

1326 The Osmanlı (Ottomans to the West), a Turkish tribal group, capture Bursa and further weaken the Byzantine Empire.

1453 The Ottomans capture Constantinople on May 29 after a two-month siege. The Byzantine Empire is extinguished.

1459 Construction of the Topkapı Palace, the heart of the Ottoman Empire, begins.

1481 Beyazıt II becomes Sultan.

1492 Beyazıt II sends an Ottoman fleet to Spain to save the Jews from persecution.

1514 Selim I "the Grim" wins a crucial victory over the Persians.

1517 Selim I captures Medina, takes the title of Caliph.

1529 The Ottomans reach the gates of Vienna led by Süleyman the Magnificent.

1558 The completion of the Süleymaniye Camii by Sinan.

1571 Don John of Austria defeats the Ottoman navy at Lepanto.

1616 The monumental Sultanahmet Camii is completed after eight years' toil.

1729 Sultan Ahmet I establishes the Ottoman Empire's first printing press.

1779 The Ottomans lose the Crimea to Russia.

1830 Greece fights off Ottoman control and becomes an independent state.

1839 Sultan Abdülmecid begins to reform the empire on European lines.

1853 Tsar Nicholas I of Russia declares the Ottoman Empire the "sick man of Europe".

1854 Florence Nightingale arrives.

1856 Abdülmecit leaves Topkapı Palace and moves to European-style Dolmabahçe Palace.

1888 Visitors from Europe reach Istanbul on the new Orient Express.

1889 Foundation of The Committee for Union and Progress (CUP) or Young Turks as they are better known.

1909 Sultan Abdülhamit deposed by the CUP.

1914 Ottoman Turkey signs an alliance with Germany and enters World War I.

1918 Britain occupies Istanbul after the Allied victory in World War I.

1919 Mustafa Kemal lands at Samsun on the Black Sea, triggering the Turkish War of Independence.

1922 The Sultanate is abolished by Turkish nationalists led by Atatürk.

1923 The Republic of Turkey is officially founded, Ankara replaces Istanbul as capital.

1934 Haghia Sophia (Aya Sofya), a church then a mosque, becomes a museum.

1938 Atatürk dies at Dolmabahçe Palace.

1939 Turkey remains neutral for most of World War II, Istanbul a centre of intrigue.

1955 A weekend of rioting destroys many Greek minority-owned properties on İstiklal Caddesi and across the city.

1960 Turkey's first military coup.

1971 Second military coup.

1977 Thirty-nine leftist demonstrators are shot by extremists at a May Day rally in Taksim Square known as "Bloody May Day" during the rise of the leftwing movement.

1980 Turkey's third military coup.

1994 A pro-Islamic Refah Party wins Istanbul in the municipal elections, Tayyip Erdoğan becomes mayor.

2002 Pro-Islamic AKP sweep to power in general elections led by Tayyip Erdoğan.

2010 Istanbul is joint European Capital of Culture.

2011 The AKP wins the general elections for a record third time.

2013 Protests erupt in Gezi Park when the government puts forward proposals to replace a green area with a new shopping mall.

2014 Tayyip Erdoğan becomes Turkey's first popularly elected president.

2015 The AKP win the general elections for the fourth time.

2016 A series of terrorist attacks in Istanbul cast a shadow over the country and there is an attempted coup.

2018 The new Istanbul Airport opens to passengers.

2019 Canal Istanbul construction begins.

2021 Turkey changes its official name to Türkiye.

2022 Terrorist bomb in Istanbul kills six.

2023 National elections see Recep Tayyip Erdoğan returned as president and his party, AKP, win the elections, their sixth victory in succession.

Turkish

Few visitors to Istanbul speak any Turkish and only a handful bother to try to learn any. This is a great shame as a very little Turkish can go a long way not only in helping you negotiate your way around the city – particularly its less visited quarters – but also in showing that you have an interest in an intensely proud people who often feel that they are misunderstood by foreigners. Below is a brief guide to pronunciation, some useful words and phrases and a basic glossary for food and drink.

Pronunciation

Turkish is phonetically spelt and, compared to most other languages, grammatically regular. It is lightly stressed, usually on the last syllable. It uses the following letters which do not appear in the English version of the Latin alphabet – ç, ğ, ı, ö, ş, ü – but does not contain the letters q, w or x. Below is a brief pronunciation guide.

Aa short a, as in car
Ee as in pet
İi as in bin
Iı an **uh** sound
Oo as in d**o**te
Öö like **ur** in ch**ur**n
Uu as in cl**ue**
Üü like **ew** in d**ew**
Cc like **j** in **j**elly
Çç like **ch** in **ch**ang
Gg like **g** as in **g**o
Ğğ hardly pronounced, but slightly lengthens the preceding vowel
Hh as in **h**ate
Jj like the **s** in trea**s**ure
Şş like **sh** in **sh**op
Vv between a **v** and a **w**

Words and phrases

Basics

good morning günaydın
good afternoon iyi günler
good evening iyi akşamlar
good night iyi geceler
hello merhaba
goodbye Allaha ısmarladık
yes evet
no hayır
no (there isn't/aren't any) yok

please lütfen
thank you teşekkür ederim/ sağol
you're welcome bir şey değil
How are you? Nasılsınız? Nasılsın?
I'm fine İyiyim
Do you speak English? İngilizce biliyormusunuz?
I don't know bilmiyorum
I beg your pardon affedersiniz
excuse me pardon
I'm English/ İngilizim/**Scottish/** Iskoçyalım/ **Irish/** Irlandalıyım/**American/** Amerikalı/ **Australian** Avustralyalım
today bugün
tomorrow yarın
yesterday dün
now şimdi
later sonra
in the morning sabahleyin
in the afternoon oğle'den sonra
in the evening akşamleyin
here/there bur(a)da/şur(a)da
over there or(a) da
good/bad iyi/kötü, fena
big/small büyük/küçük
cheap/expensive ucuz/pahalı
early/late erken/geç
hot/cold sıcak/soğuk
near/far yakın/uzak
vacant/occupied boş/dolu
Mr Bey (follows first name)
Miss Bayan (precedes first name)
Mrs Hanım (follows first name)

Questions and directions

Where is the...? ...Nerede?
When? Ne zaman?
What/What is it? Ne/ne dir?
How much Ne kadar/kaç para?**(does it cost?)**
How many? Kaç tane?
What time is it? Saat kaç?
How do I get to...? ...'a/e nasıl giderim?
How far is it to...? ...'a/e ne kadar uzak?
When does it open? Saat kaçta açılıyor?
When does it close? Saat kaçta kapanıyor?

Transport

aeroplane uçak
bus otobüs
train tren
car araba
taxi taksi
ferry feribot, vapur
catamaran, sea bus deniz otobüsü
bus station otogar
railway station gar, tren ıstasyonu
ferry terminal/jetty iskele
A ticket to... ...'a bir bilet
one-way gidiş sadece
return gidiş-dönüş
What time does it leave? Saat kaçta kalkıyor?
Where does it leave from? Nereden kalkıyor?

Signs

açık/kapalı open/closed
baylar gentlemen
bayanlar ladies
çekiniz/itiniz pull/push
dikkat beware
dur stop, halt
giriş/çıkış entrance/exit
girmek yasaktır entry forbidden
ilk yardım first aid
lütfen ayakkabılarınızı çıkartınız please take off your shoes
sigara içilmez no smoking
WC/tuvalet WC

Accommodation

hotel otel
pension pansiyon
Do you have a room? Boş odanız var mı?
single/double/triple Tek/çift/üç kişilik
with a double bed fransiz yataklı
with a shower duşlu
hot water sıcak su
cold water soğuk su
Can I see it? Bakabilirmiyim?
I have a booking Reservasyonum var
Is there wi-fi? Kablosuz internet var mı?
What's the password? Şifre nedir?

Numbers

bir 1
iki 2
üç 3
dört 4
beş 5

altı 6
yedi 7
sekiz 8
dokuz 9
on 10
on bir 11
on iki 12
on üç 13
yirmi 20
otuz 30
kırk 40
elli 50
altmış 60
yetmiş 70
seksen 80
doksan 90
yüz 100
yüz kırk 140
iki yüz 200
yedi yüz 700
bin 1000

Food and drink terms

Basics

bal honey
buz ice
ekmek bread
makarna pasta (noodles)
peynir cheese
pilav, pirinç rice
şeker sugar
su water
süt milk
tereyağı butter
tuz salt
zeytin yağı olive oil
yoğurt yoghurt
yumurta eggs

Cooking terms

acı hot, spicy
ezme puréed dip
fırında(n) baked
haşlama stew(ed)
ızgarada(n) grilled
sıcak/soğuk hot/cold (meze)
soslu, salçalı in red sauce
tava, sahanda deep-fried, fried
yoğurtlu in yoghurt sauce

zeytinyağlılar cold cooked vegetables with olive oil
with/without (meat) (et)li/(et)siz

Soup (çorba)

ezo gelin tomato, rice and lentil
işkembe tripe
mercimek lentil
tarhana yoghurt, grain and spice
tavuk chicken

Appetizers (meze)

Antep or acılı ezmesi spicy tomato/ chilli mash
cacık yoghurt, cucumber and herb dip
çoban salatası tomato, cucumber, parsley, pepper and onion salad
haydarı strained yoghurt and garlic dip
imam bayıldı cold baked aubergine, onion and tomato
mücver courgette fritters
patlıcan ezmesi aubergine pâté
piyaz white haricots, onions and parsley salad
sigara böreği cheese-filled pastry rolls
turşu pickled vegetables
yaprak dolması rice-stuffed vine leaves
zeytin olives

Meat (et) dishes

adana kebap spicy mincemeat kebab on skewer
beyti minced kebab in flatbread
çiğ köfte spicy bulgur patties
ciğer liver
dana eti beef
döner kebap meat sliced from a rotisserie
İskender kebap döner in yoghurt and tomato sauce
kanat chicken wing
karışık ızgara mixed grill
köfte meatballs
kuzu lamb
şiş kebap shish kebab, lamb or chicken
tavuk/piliç chicken

Snack/lunch foods

börek pastry with cheese, meat or potato filling
çerez nut and roasted pulse nibbles

gözleme stuffed paratha-like flatbread
lahmacun flatbread with spicy mincemeat
mantı Turkish "ravioli" in yoghurt sauce
midye dolması rice-stuffed mussels
pide Turkish "pizza"
poğaça soft, often filled, bread roll
simit bread rings studded with sesame seeds

Fish (balik) and seafood (deniz ürünleri)

barbunya/tekir red mullet, small/ large
çipura gilt-head bream
hamsi anchovy (Black Sea)
kalamar squid
kalkan turbot
karides prawns
kılıç swordfish
levrek sea bass
lüfer bluefish
mercan pandora/red bream
mezgit whitebait
palamut/torik small/large bonito
sardalya sardine

Vegetables (sebze)

bamya okra, lady's fingers
biber peppers
domates tomato
ıspanak spinach
kabak courgette
mantar mushrooms
maydanoz parsley
nohut chickpeas
patates potato
patlıcan aubergine
roka, tere rocket greens
salatalık cucumber
soğan onion
taze fasulye French beans

Fruit (meyve) and nuts (fistik)

antep fıstığı pistachio
armut pear
badem almond
ceviz walnut
çilek strawberry
elma apple

erik plum
fındık hazlenut
incir fig
karpuz watermelon
kayısı apricot
kiraz sweet cherry
muz banana
nar pomegranate
portakal orange
şeftali peach
üzüm grape
vişne sour cherry

Cheese

beyaz white goat's cheese, like feta
kaşar yellow cow's cheese
otlu peynir herb-stuffed goat's cheese
tulum goat's cheese cured in a goatskin

Sweets (tatilar) and pastries (pastalar)

acı badem giant almond biscuit
baklava nut-filled filo pastry
dondurma ice cream
helva sweet made from semolina flour
İrmik helvası semolina and nut helva
kabak tatlısı baked pumpkin served with tahini
kadayıf "shredded wheat" in syrup
lokum Turkish delight
muhallebi milk pudding with rice flour and rosewater
sütlaç rice pudding
tahin helvası sesame paste helva
tavuk göğsü chicken-breast, milk, sugar and rice taffy

Drinks

ayran drinking yoghurt
bira beer
çay tea
elma çayı hot apple-flavoured drink
kahve coffee
maden suyu/soda mineral water (fizzy)
meyva suyu fruit juice
rakı aniseed-flavoured spirit
şarap wine

SMALL PRINT

Publishing Information
Fifth Edition 2024

Distribution
UK, Ireland and Europe
Apa Publications (UK) Ltd; sales@roughguides.com
United States and Canada
Ingram Publisher Services; ips@ingramcontent.com
Australia and New Zealand
Booktopia; retailer@booktopia.com.au
Worldwide
Apa Publications (UK) Ltd; sales@roughguides.com

Special Sales, Content Licensing and CoPublishing
Rough Guides can be purchased in bulk quantities at discounted prices. We can create special editions, personalised jackets and corporate imprints tailored to your needs. sales@roughguides.com.
roughguides.com

Printed in Czech Republic

This book was produced using **Typefi** automated publishing software.

A catalogue record for this book is available from the British Library
The publishers and authors have done their best to ensure the accuracy and currency of all the information in **Pocket Rough Guide Istanbul**, however, they can accept no responsibility for any loss, injury, or inconvenience sustained by any traveller as a result of information or advice contained in the guide.

Rough Guide Credits
Editor: Kate Drynan
Cartography: Katie Bennett
Picture Editor: Tom Smyth
Layout: Pradeep Thapliyal
Original design: Richard Czapnik
Head of DTP and Pre-Press: Rebeka Davies
Head of Publishing: Sarah Clark

Acknowledgements
The author would like to thank Erkan Karpus (Talisman Tour) and Sinan Sokmen (Istanbul Studio) for all their help.

Help us update

We've gone to a lot of effort to ensure that this edition of the **Pocket Rough Guide Istanbul** is accurate and up-to-date. However, things change – places get "discovered", opening hours are notoriously fickle, restaurants and rooms raise prices or lower standards. If you feel we've got it wrong or left something out, we'd like to know, and if you can remember the address, the price, the hours, the phone number, so much the better.

Please send your comments with the subject line "**Pocket Rough Guide Istanbul Update**" to mail@uk.roughguides.com. We'll credit all contributions and send a copy of the next edition (or any other Rough Guide if you prefer) for the very best emails.

Photo Credits

(Key: T-top; C-centre; B-bottom; L-left; R-right)

Ahmet Gülkokan/Hiç-Contemporary Crafts 90
Alamy 70, 71, 75, 76, 104, 110, 117
Four Seasons Hotels and Resorts 132/133
Getty Images 15B, 51
iStock 11T, 16B, 18T, 21T, 31, 34, 43, 88, 100, 126/127
Lydia Evans/Rough Guides 4, 12/13B, 17B, 17T, 18B, 20T, 20C, 30, 37, 38, 39, 41, 48, 52, 56, 58, 64, 66, 67, 73, 80, 81, 83, 85, 92, 95, 101, 103, 105, 106, 108, 116, 121, 123, 124, 131

Mini Müzikhol 111
Murat Germen/Istanbul Modern 13C
Ottoman Hotels Group 40
Pera Palace Hotel 21B
Roger d'Olivere Mapp/Rough Guides 12/13T, 14T, 16T, 19B, 20B, 21C, 25, 47, 63, 77, 98, 113, 129
Shutterstock 1, 2T, 2BL, 2C, 2BR, 6, 10, 11B, 12BL, 14B, 15T, 18C, 19T, 19C, 22/23, 33, 35, 36, 50, 53, 54, 55, 65, 69, 82, 89, 119, 126, 142/143
Turkish Culture and Tourism Office 28

Cover: Süleymaniye Mosque **ihsan Gercelman/Shutterstock**

Index

INDEX

NOTES